# The State of North Carolina with Native American Ancestry

### The Formation of the Eastern and Coastal Counties in North Carolina

## Milton E. Campbell

Order this book online at www.trafford.com
or email orders@trafford.com

Most Trafford titles are also available at major online book retailers.

© Copyright 2011 Milton Campbell, Ph.D.

All rights reserved. No part of this publication may be reproduced, stored in a retrieval system, or transmitted, in any form or by any means, electronic, mechanical, photocopying, recording, or otherwise, without the written prior permission of the author.

Printed in the United States of America.

ISBN: 978-1-4269-5745-1 (sc)
ISBN: 978-1-4269-5746-8 (hc)
ISBN: 978-1-4269-5747-5 (e)

Library of Congress Control Number: 2011902018

Trafford rev. 05/04/2011

 www.trafford.com

North America & international
toll-free: 1 888 232 4444 (USA & Canada)
phone: 250 383 6864 ♦ fax: 812 355 4082

# Contents

| | | |
|---|---|---|
| Acknowledgments | | ix |
| Introduction | | xi |
| Chapter I | Early History of the state of North Carolina | 1 |
| Chapter II | The Formation of Coastal and Eastern Counties in North Carolina | 11 |
| Chapter III | History of American Indians living in the interior of the American Southwest | 33 |
| Chapter IV | Coharie Indians Tribe who descend from the Neusiok Indians | 35 |
| Chapter V | Cherokee Indian from the Southern United States | 39 |
| Chapter VI | Lumbee Indians are descendants of the Cheraw and Siouan speaking tribes | 53 |
| Chapter VII | Haliwa-Soponi Indians from Halifax and Warren Counties | 59 |
| Chapter VIII | Occaneechi Indian are related to the Saponi and Tutelo | 63 |
| Chapter IX | Meherrin Indian Tribe is of the same linguistic stock as the Cherokee and Tuscarora | 67 |
| Chapter X | Tuscarora Indian Tribe | 69 |

| | | |
|---|---|---|
| Chapter XI | Waccamaw Siouan Indians are located in Bladen and Columbus counties | 73 |
| Chapter XII | Surnames: Campbell, Graham, Jacobs, Spaulding, Blanks, and Moore. | 79 |
| Chapter XIII | Native American Ancestry | 105 |
| Conclusions | | 111 |
| Endnotes | | 113 |

The Formation of the State of North Carolina Coastal and Eastern Counties During the Period of 1663-1808 and the Native American Ancestry

Milton E. Campbell

# Acknowledgments

*It is a great challenge to begin listing those who have contributed to the production of this document. It is the fear that someone may be over looked who has contributed to this extensive research. I being, by expressing my deep and abiding appreciation to four people who encouraged me to continue to preserve family history, my grandmother Mrs. Mattie Spaulding Campbell, my great uncle Mr. Dow Spaulding and two of my great –aunts Mrs. Agnes Spaulding Hill and Mrs. Carrie Spaulding Wilson. Although they are no longer with us on earth, I know that there spirit live.*

*I owe debt of gratitude to Mr. Wendell Campbell, who aided in the collecting of photographs and personal interviews for this book and his graphic design experience which made this project a success. My research would never have been completed without the ongoing assistance of Mr. Campbell.*

*I am also in debt to many of the families who have given personal interviews and have preserved their family written and oral Native American Ancestry. Specifically speaking, the Campbell's, Blanks, Moore's, Mitchells, Grahams, Jacobs, Sanderson's, Locklears, Oxendines and Spaulding families.*

*Finally, special appreciation expressed to the staff of the North Carolina Division of Archives and History in Raleigh. Without the state archival records this project would not have been possible.*

# Introduction

*Before the dying of the last great ice age, a land bridge existed between what is now Russia and Alaska. Due to the tremendous amount of ice and snow, which built up during the ice age, caused the seas to recede and leave this land bridge. Across this low lying plain wandered many tribes that eventually became American Indians. The migrations across the land strip continued at intervals until the sea rose up and covered the passage. Gradually, as more and more tribes of wandering hunters came to the new land, they spread south and west and began to prosper. They learned to make better clothes, to guard against the still cold winters, to build better shelters and to find better caves, in which to live. When the first series of Asiatic men wandered out of Asia and on to the North American continent, a great part of what is now the Western States was a vast plain that had once been an inland sea. Upon these plain-grazed animals, that provided sufficient food for these wandering tribes. As time passed, and the numbers of men gradually increased, it became very difficult for all to find enough wild meat to satisfy their needs. Some turned to gathering fruits and berries and others turned to finding ways to trap fish and other aquatic life.*

*Down through the great plains of the west and Old Mexico, gradually moved the forerunners of what we now call the Aztec and Mayan people. These tribes-found an environment, which they no longer had to spend every waking hour in search of enough food to keep from starving. Therefore, they had time to use their brains to begin to solve the mysteries of the earth and mankind. They began to constructed permanent villages, which were usually located near streams. Also, the Cherokees were among the Southeastern Indians, who had developed a complex way of living by the time the first white man touched the United States. They built houses, wove cloth, made vessels of clay and most important of all, organized into a loosely- knit confederation.*

*The first travelers who came in contact with the tribes of Indians who lived along the eastern half of the United States did not make detailed studies of their cultures. Basically, they observed and recorded their outward acts but did not give a studied report on the whys and wherefores of these actions. Consequently, the only way we have of knowing their affairs is by judging form the things they left and by the reports of later travelers who did really observe and record their findings.*

*Once white settlers had seen the vast untamed wilderness of America, the fate of the Indian was sealed. The white men first came in small parties with pretensions of friendliness to the Indians. Afterward, they came in larger parties with more gear and less friendliness. At first, white settlers were mostly met with curiosity and awe, but then, after more and more came to build cabins and fences, upon what had once been fertile forests and untamed wilderness, the Indians began to resist and to wonder where it would all end. The American Indians asked the officials of the colonies to hold back the ever-swelling tide to certain boundaries, and when this failed, they began to try to stem the tide, as they had in other times with their own kind. Indian warfare was not of a kind the colonist had ever known before. It was a savage and ruthless war that left women and children in villages and towns without protection or mercy.*

*For nearly a hundred years after the visit of Desoto, the Cherokees had very little contact with white men. The first known contact the British Settlements had with the Cherokee occurred at Richmond, Virginia. The first known English settlement of South Carolina occurred in 1670 and the first known treat signed by a Cherokee chief occurred in 1684. By the early seventeen hundreds, regular skirmished were occurring between the races.*

*Between the years 1700 and 1763, the different tribes that lay between the Spanish, French, and English colonies were political pawns for the different interests of the various nations. One major difference existed between the way the English treated the Indians and the way the Spanish and French treated them. The French, particularly, mingled and mixed with them freely. Their traders often married Indian women and settled down within the tribes to continue to serve their mother country as well as being a part of the Indian tribal life. The English did this very seldom. They looked down on the Indians' way of life and associated with them only when forced to. The frontiersmen feared and hated the Indians and lost few opportunities to do them harm. By the time the American Revolution broke out in 1776, the Indians were firmly aligned against the Frontier Americans. To the Native American Indians, the British Government stood as the only symbol of authority. They were well aware that they could expect very little quarter from the frontier government. By the latter part of 1776, the Indians and Tories began attacking the frontier settlements all along the coast of South Carolina and Georgia.*

*British forces, with the active assistance of their Indian allies, had by the early part of 1780 taken all of Georgia and South Carolina. Their armies were preparing to move northward into North Carolina and Virginia when they made the mistake of demanding the surrender of the mountain men who up to this time had spent their efforts in fighting off the Indian allies of the British. The mountain men assembled, and under leadership of their own choosing, began the march of King's Mountain, South Carolina, that spelled the defeat of the British in the South. After burning of the Indians towns and the defeat of the British at King's Mountain left the Cherokee at the mercy of the frontier Americans.*

*Andrew Jackson, himself a frontiersman, aided the forces in Georgia that finally pushed the Indians off their lands. When Georgia annexed the Cherokee lands and the Supreme Court of the United States ruled against them, it was Jackson who said, "The Court has made its decision now let them enforce it."*

*It was also Jackson's life that had been saved by a great Cherokee by the name of Junaluska at the Battle of Horse Shoe Bend. Although many people spoke up for the rights of the Tribe in the United Sates Congress and in editorial comment, their forces were not strong enough to force the cancellation of the treaty, which stipulated they were to be removed by May 26, 1838.*

*Although English records of the period show that the Indians of the Carolinas had been wiped out, this was a mistaken notion based on wishful thinking and other errors. This particular area where remnants of Waccamaw, Cape Fear, and other Siouan tribes lived is designated by Patricia Lerch in Political History of the Waccamaw Sioux, 1900-1983, as the lowlands four miles north of Bolton including Brown Marsh, White Marsh, and Lake Waccamaw. It spreads westward in Columbus County beyond Whiteville and northward into Bladen County. To prove that Peedee, Catawba, etc., survived and that their remnants still play a large part in the existing population of the Mitchell, Moores, Spaulding Family, one might consult the South Carolina B.P.R.O. (223). This document says that the northern Indians were estimated in 1717 to contain a total of "2800" souls of which number there is left about 1000 men..." That the Peedee and Waccamaw Indians were not destroyed can be proved by a number of references such as the Council Record Journal for 1717 (I: 21 and XVI: 409), South Carolina B.P.R.O. (VIII: 25-26), Mooney (61-62) and Milling (218).*

*The author intent is to show the survival of the Native American Indians existence in the 21st century in the state of North Carolina. After giving the reader a brief overview on the history of North Carolina, he further discuss the state population, United States Census Reports, Geography, Native Indians, Permanent Settlement, Colonial Period, Antebellum Period, Civil War in North Carolina. The author discusses the first Europeans Settlements and Bath, the first town in North Carolina. Afterward, discussion on the establishment of some of the earliest counties within the state (New Hanover, Bladen, Columbus, Brunswick, Robeson, Cumberland, Orange, Duplin, Anson), the author make a special attempt to establish the survival of the Native Americans in each county.*

*The first United States Census Report in 1790, and in other census reports between 1790-1900 Native American were classified as mulatto's and black. Many Native American had no say in how they were classified by the United States government. The author intent is to correct this unjust discrimination placed on the identity of the Native American families in North Carolina. There is attempt to identify the origin and make a historical significance to the Native American Ancestry of the Spaulding's, Mitchells, Moore's, Jacobs, Blanks, Grahams, Campbell families). These families originated in Eastern North Carolina and were predominantly of the Siouan tribe and live today in what is known as Bladen and Columbus counties. However, in the 1880 Census we see George Spaulding who had moved from Columbus County to Roberson County and married into Croatan tribe. It must be stated in my research there were many Spaulding family members that had married into other Native American tribes beside the Siouan. Other tribes in which the Spaulding family married into pre and post civil war were the Cherokee and Tuscarora.*

# CHAPTER I

## *Early History of the state of North Carolina*

North Carolina is a state located on the Atlantic Seaboard in the southeastern United States. The state borders South Carolina and Georgia to the south, Tennessee to the west and Virginia to the north. North Carolina contains 100 counties and its capital is located in Raleigh.

The state of North Carolina was one of the original Thirteen Colonies, originally know as Carolina. Joara, a native village near present-day Morganton, was the site in 1567 of Fort San Juan, the first Spanish colonial settlement in the interior of what became the United States. (1) A colony was later established at Roanoke Island, the first attempt by the English to found a settlement in the Americas. (2)

North Carolina was one of the last of the Confederate states to declare secession from the Union on May 20, 1861. However, it was restored on July 4, 1868. The state of North Carolina was the location of the first successful controlled, powered and sustained havier-than-air flight, by the Wright brothers, at Kill Devil Hills, about 7 miles from Kitty Hawk in 1903.

Presently, North Carolina is a fast-growing state with an increasingly diverse economy and population. As of August 1, 2008, the population was estimated to be 9,222,465. (3) Recognizing eight Native American tribes, North Carolina has the largest population of Native Americans of any state east of the Mississippi River.

*Milton E. Campbell*

## Geography

*The state of North Carolina consists of three main geographic sections: the coastal plain, which occupies the eastern 45% of the state; the Piedmont region, which contains the middle 35%; and the Appalachian Mountains and foothills. The extreme eastern section of the state contains the Outer Banks, a string of sandy, narrow islands, which form a barrier between the Atlantic Ocean and inland waterways. The Outer Banks form two sounds the Albemarle Sound in the north and Pamlico Sound in the south. They are two largest landlocked sounds in the United States.*

## Native Americans, Lost Colonies and Permanent Settlement

*Many different native peoples, including those of the ancient Mississippian culture established by 1000 A.D. in the Piedmont, originally inhabited North Carolina. Historically documented tribes included Cherokee, Tuscarora, Cheraw, Pamlico, Meherrin, Coree, Machapunga, Cape Fear Indians, Waxham, Saponi, Tutelo, Waccamaw, Coharie, and Catawba.*

*Spanish explorers traveling inland encountered the last of the Mississippian culture at Joara, near present-day Morganton. Records of Hernando De Soto attested to his meeting with them in 1540. In 1567 Captain Juan Pardo led an expedition into the interior of North Carolina on a journey to claim the area for the Spanish colony, as well as establish another route to protect silver mines in Mexico. (4) Pardo made a winter base at Joara, which he renamed Cuenca. The expedition built Fort San Juan and left 30 men, while Pardo traveled further, establishing five other forts. He returned by a different route to Santa Elena on Parris Island, South Carolina, then a center of Spanish Florida. In the spring of 1568, natives killed all the soldiers and burned the six forts in the interior, including the one at Fort San Juan. The Spanish never turned to the interior to press their colonial claims, but this marked the first European attempt at colonization of the interior of what became the United States. (5.6)*

*In 1584, Elizabeth I granted a charter to Sir Walter Raleigh, for who the state capital is named, for land in present-day North Carolina (then Virginia). (7) Raleigh established two colonies on the coast in the late 1580s, both ending in failure. It was the second American territory the British attempted to colonize. The demise of one, the "Lost Colony" of Roanoke Island, remains one of the great mysteries of American history. Virginia Dare, the first English child to be born in North America, was born on Roanoke Island on August 18, 1587. Dare County is name for her.*

*As early as 1650, colonists from the Virginia Colony moved into the area of Albermale Sound. By 1663, King Charles II of England granted a charter to start a new Colony on the North American continent, which generally established its borders. He name it Carolina in honor of his father Charles I. (8) By 1665, a second charter was issued to attempt to resolve territorial questions. In 1710, due to disputes over governance, the Carolina colony began a split into North Carolina and South Carolina. This latter became a crown colony in 1729.*

## Colonial Period and Revolutionary War

*The first permanent European settlers of North Carolina were British colonists who migrated south from Virginia, following a rapid growth of the colony and the subsequent shortage of available farmland. Nathaniel Batts was documented as one of the first of these Virginian migrants. He settled south of the Chowan River and east of the Great Dismal Swamp in 1655. (9) By 1663, this northeastern area of the Province of Carolina, known as the Albermarle Settlements, was undergoing full-scale British settlement. (10) During the same period, the English monarch Charles II gave the province to the Lords Proprietors, a group of noblemen who had helped restore Charles to the throne in 1660. The new province of "Carolina" was named in honor and memory of King Charles I. In the year of 1712 North Carolina became a separate colony. With the exception of the Earl Granville holdings, it became a royal colony seventeen years later. (11)*

*Differences in the settlement patterns of eastern and western North Carolina, or the low country and uplands, affected the political, economic, and social life of the state from the eighteenth until the twentieth century. Chiefly immigrants from England and the Scottish Highlands settled the Tidewater in eastern North Carolina. Mostly Scots-Irish and German Protestants, the so-called "cohee", settled the upcountry of western North Carolina. Arriving during the mid-to late 18$^{th}$ century, the Scots-Irish from Ireland were the largest immigrant group before the Revolution. During the Revolutionary War, the English and Highland Scots of eastern North Carolina tended to remain loyal to the British Crown, because of longstanding business and personal connections with Great Britain. The Scots-Irish and German settlers of western North Carolina tended to favor American independence from Britain.*

*Most of the English colonists arrived as indentured servants, hiring themselves out as laborers for a fixed period to pay for their passage. In the early years the line between indentured servants and African slaves or laborers was fluid. Some Africans were allowed to earn their freedom before slavery became a life long status. Most of the free colored families formed in North Carolina before the Revolution were descended from relationships or marriages between free white women and enslaved or free African or African-American men. However, there is evidence that White Men also had relationship with free women of color and also white men had relationships with Indian Women. Many had migrated or were descendants of migrants from colonial Virginia. (12) As the flow of indentured laborers to the colony decreased with improving economics condition in Great Britain, more slaves were imported and the state's restrictions on slavery hardened. The economy's growth and prosperity was base on slave labor, devoted first to the production of tobacco.*

*On April 12, 1776, the colony became the first to instruct its delegates to the Continental Congress to vote for independence form British crown, through the Halifax Resolves passed by the North Carolina Provincial Congress. The dates for both of these independence-related events are memorialized on the state flag and state seal. (13) Throughout the*

Revolutionary War, fierce guerilla warfare erupted between bands of pro-independence and pro-British colonists. In some cases the war was also an excuse to settle private grudged and rivalries. A Major American victory in the war took place at King's Mountain along the North Carolina-South Carolina border. On October 7, 1780 a force of 1000 mountain men from western North Carolina, which include what is today the State of Tennessee, overwhelmed a force of some 1000 British troops led by Major Patrick Ferguson. Most of the British soldiers in the battle were Carolinians who had remained loyal to the British Crown. The American victory at Kings Mountain gave the advantage to colonists who favored American independence, and prevented the British Army from recruiting new soldiers from the Tories.

The road to Yorktown and America's independence from Great Britain led through North Carolina. As the British Army moved north from victories in Charleston and Camden, South Carolina, the Southern Division of the Continental Army and local militia prepared to meet them. Following General Daniel Morgan's victory over the British Cavalry Commander Banastre Tarleton at the Battle of Cowpens on January 17, 1781, southern commander Nathanael Greene led British Lord Charles Cornwallis across the heartland of North Carolina, and away from Cornwallis's base of supply in Charleston, South Carolina. This campaign is known as "The Race to the Dan" or " The Race for the River."(11)

Generals Greene and Cornwallis finally met at the Battle of Guilford Courthouse in present-day Greensboro on March 15, 1781. Although the British troops held the field at the end of the battle, their casualties at the hands of the numerically superior American Army were crippling. Following this "Pyhrric victory, Cornwallis chose to move to the Virginia coastline to get reinforcements, and to allow the Royal Navy to protect his battered army. This decision would result in Cornwallis's eventual defeat at Yorktown, Virginia later in 1781. The Patriots' victory there guaranteed American independence.

Milton E. Campbell

## *Antebellum Period*

The State of North Carolina became the twelfth state to ratify the Constitution on November 21, 1789. The state capitol building was completed in 1840 and is located in Raleigh, North Carolina. The majority of North Carolina's slave owners and large plantations were located in eastern portion of the state. Although North Carolina's plantation system was smaller and less cohesive than those of South Carolina, Virginia, or Georgia, there were significant numbers of planters concentrated in the counties around the port cities of Wilmington and Edenton, as well as suburban planters around the cities of Raleigh, Charlotte and Durham. Planters owning large estates wielded significant political and socio-economic power in antebellum North Carolina, often to the derision of the generally non-slave holding "yeoman" farmers of Western North Carolina. In mid-century, the state's rural and commercial areas were connected by the construction of a 129 mile wooden plank road, known as a "farmer's railroad," from Fayetteville in the east to Bethania (northwest of Winston-Salem). (11)

It must be stated that there were a number of free people of color in the state. Most were descended from free African Americans who had migrated along with neighbors from Virginia during the eighteenth century. Also there were free African Americans who married or had relationships with Indians and Caucasians. This can be seen all across the state, however, specifically in the Bladen and Columbus and Roberson County areas. After the Revolution, Quakers and Mennonites worked to persuade slaveholders to free their slaves. Enough were inspired by their efforts and the language of men rights, and arranged for manumission of their slaves. The number of free people of color rose in the first couple of decades after the Revolution. (14)

The Wilmington and Raleigh Railroad began construction on October 25, 1836, which allow the connection of the port city of Wilmington with the state capital of Raleigh.(15) In 1849, the North Carolina Railroad was created by act of the legislature to extend that railroad west to Greensboro, High Point, and Charlotte. During the Civil War the Wilmington-to-Raleigh stretch of the railroad would be vital to the Confederate war effort; supplies shipped into Wilmington would be moved by rail through Raleigh to the Confederate capital of Richmond, Virginia.

During the antebellum period North Carolina was overwhelmingly rural state, even by Southern standards. In 1860 only one North Carolina town, the port city of Wilmington, had a population of more than 10,000. Raleigh, the state capital, had barely more than 5,000 residents.

While slaveholding was slightly less concentrated than some Southern states, according to the 1860 census, more than 330, 000 or 33% of the population of 992,622 were enslaved African-Americans. They lived and worked chiefly on plantations in the eastern Tidewater. In addition, 30 free families, 463 free people of color lived in the state. They were also concentrated in the eastern coastal plain, especially at port cities such as Wilmington and New Bern where they had access to a variety of jobs. Free African Americans were allowed to vote until 1835, when the state rescinded their suffrage.

## American Civil War

In 1860 North Carolina was a slave state and did not vote to join the Confederacy until President Abraham Lincoln called on it to invade it sister-state, South Carolina, becoming the last or second to last state to officially join the Confederacy. The title of "last to join the Confederacy" has been disputed because Tennessee informally seceded on May 7, 1861, making North Carolina the last to secede on May 20, 1861. (16.17) However, the Tennessee legislature did not formally vote secedes until June 8, 1861. (18)

North Carolina was the site of few battles, but it provided at least 125,000 troops to the Confederacy, which was far more than any other state. Approximately 40,000 of those troops never returned home, dying of disease, battlefield wounds, and starvation. North Carolina also supplied about 15,000 Union troops. (19) Elected in

1862, Governor Zebulon Baird Vance tried to maintain state autonomy against Confederate President Jefferson Davis in Richmond.

Even after secession, some North Carolinians refused to support the Confederacy. This was particularly true on non-slave-owning farmers in the state's mountains and western Piedmont region. Some of these farmers remained neutral during the war, while some covertly supported the Union cause during the conflict. Approximately 2,000 North Carolinas from western North Carolina enlisted in the Union Army and fought for the North in the war, and two additional Union Army regiments were raised in the coastal areas of the state that were occupied by Union forces in 1862 and 1863. Even so, confederate troops from all parts of North Carolina served virtually all the major battles of the Army of Northern Virginia, the Confederacy's most famous army. The largest battle fought in North Carolina was at Bentonville, which was a futile attempt by Confederate Joseph Johnston to slow Union General William Tecumseh Sherman's advance through the Carolinas in the spring 1863. (11) In April 1865 after losing the Battle of Morrisville, Johnston surrendered to Sherman at Bennett Place, in what is to today called Durham, North Carolina. This was the last Confederate port to fall to the Union. It fell in the spring of 1865 after the nearby Second Battle of Fort Fisher.

The first Confederate soldier to be killed in the Civil War was Private Henry Wyatt, a North Carolinians. He was killed in the Battle of Big Bethel in June 1861. At the Battle of Gettysburg in July 1863; the 26th North Carolina Regiment participated in Pickett/Pettigrew's Charge and advanced the farthest into the Northern lines of any Confederate regiment. During the Battle of Chickamauga the 58th North Carolina Regiment advanced farther than any other regiment on Snodgrass Hill to push back the remaining Union forces from the battlefield. At Appomattox Court House in Virginia in April 1865, the 75th North Carolina Regiment, a cavalry unit, fired the last shots of the Confederate Army of Northern Virginia in the Civil War. For many years, North Carolinians proudly boasted that they had been "First at Bethel, Farthest at Gettysburg and Chickamauga, and Last at Appomattox."

## 2007 United States Census Report from the state of North Carolina

In 2007, the United States Census estimated that the racial makeup of North Carolina was as follows: 70% White American, 25.3% African American, 1.2% American Indians, and the remaining 6.5 % are Hispanic or Latino. North Carolina has historically been a rural state, with most of the population living on farms or in small towns. However, over the last 35 years the state has undergone rapid urbanization, and today most of North Carolina's residents live in urban and suburban areas, as in the case in most of the United States. In particular, the cities of Charlotte and Raleigh have become major urban centers, with large, diverse, mainly affluent and rapidly growing populations. Immigrants from Latin America, India, and Southeast Asia have fueled most of this growth in diversity. (20)

## 2008 United States Census Report from the State of North Carolina

The United States Census Bureau, as of July1, 2008, estimated North Carolina's population at 9,222,414, which represents an increase of 1,175,914, or 14.6%, since the last census in 2000. This exceeds the rate of growth for the United States as a whole. The growth comprises a natural increase since the last census of 412,906 people (that is 1,015,065 births minus 602,159 deaths) and increase due to net migration of 783,382 people into the state. Immigration from outside the United States resulted in a net increase of 192,099 people, and migration within the country produced a net gain of 591,283 people. Between 2005 and 2006, North Carolina, passed New Jersey to become the 10th most populous state. The state's population reported as under 5 years old was 6.7%, 24.2% were under 18, and 12.0% were 65 or older. Females made up approximately 51% of the population.

# Chapter II

## *The Formation of Coastal and Eastern Counties in North Carolina*

### European Americans

Settled first, the coastal region attracted primarily English immigrants of the early migrations, including indentured servants transported to the colonies and descendants of English who migrated from Virginia. In addition, there were waves of Protestant European immigration, including the British, Scots, Irish, French Huguenots, and Swiss Germans who settled New Bern, North Carolina. (21) Many Pennsylvania Germans came down the Shenandoah Valley on the Great Wagon Road and settled in the western Piedmont and the foothills of the Blue Ridge. A concentration of Welsh along with others from Britain and Ireland settled east of present day Fayetteville in the 18th century.

### Bath the first town established in North Carolina

In the year of 1663 North Carolina was granted to eight of the political friends of King Charles II of England. The Lords Proprietors of Carolina, promoted the settlement of this state. In the year of 1690 there were more settlers arriving in the state on the Pamlico River. In 1696 the county of Bath was established and in 1705 the present Beaufort County was established as Pampticough Precinct. The first town in North Carolina was called Bath and it was established in 1705. (22) Bath was also the haunt of Edward Teach, better known as Blackbeard. He is to have married a local girl and briefly settled

Milton E. Campbell

in the harbor town around 1716. Legends has that Blackbeard struck bargains in Bath with Royal Governor Charles Eden. Also, with the establishment of the State of North Carolina came plantations and slaves. Among the earlier plantations found in North Carolina were the John Woodard Senior Plantation established in 1765 and the same family established another plantation in 1785. . The Benjamin Blount, Jr. Plantations in which four slaves were listed in his will and later Reading and Lucy Blount Plantation established in 1817. (23)

Some of the first Immigrants to Bath County, North Carolina were the following family and they brought from 10 to 20 persons with them too the state between 1695-1702. William Glover, John White, Farnifould Green, William Barrow, Joseph Ming, Nathaniel Chevin, Richard Smith, James Nevill, Thomas Dearham, Thomas Jones, Peter Godfrey, Thomas Worsley, Henry Lockey, Thomas Lepper, John Nellson Jr., William Brice. All of these people brought to North Carolina were of European Descent except two brought by Thomas Jones one was a Negro and another was an Indian women name Betty. Bath County covered a mass territory from the coast of North Carolina until it joins New Hanover Precinct, the present day New Hanover County, North Carolina. Bath County was abolished in 1739 and all of its constituent precincts became counties.

In Beaufort County, North Carolina today there is a town call Bath with a population of 275 as reported in the 2000 census. It is the not only the oldest town in North Carolina but it was the first capital of the state and port of entry. The town of Bath is 305 years old and is full of rich history. Bath is located is North Carolina's coastal plains region. The racial makeup of the town is 95.64 % white, 2.91 % African American, 1.09% Native American.(24)

## House of Hanover

The House of Hanover is a Germanic royal dynasty, which has ruled the Duchy of Brunswick-Luneburg, the Kingdom of Hanover and the Kingdom of Great Britain and the Kingdom of Ireland. It succeeded the House Stuart as monarchs of Great Britain and Ireland in 1714 and held that office until the death of Victoria in 1901. They are sometimes referred to as the House of Brunswick and Luneburg, Hanover line. The house of Hanover is a younger branch of the House of Welf, which in turn is the senior branch of the House of Este, with all three being offshoots of the ancient Saxon House of Wettin.

Queen Victoria was the granddaughter of George, III, and was a descendant of most major European royal houses. She arranged marriages for her children and grandchildren across the continent, typing Europe together: this earned her nickname "the grandmother of Europe." She was the last British monarch of the House of Hanover; her son King Edward VII belonged to the House of Saxe-Coburg and Gotha since she could not inherit the German kingdom and duchies under Salic law. Those possessions passed to the next eligible male heir, her uncle Ernest Augustus I of Hanover, the Duke of Cumberland and Teviotdale- the fifth son of George III. In the United Kingdom, after World War I, King George V changed the house's name from SaxeCoburg and Gotha to the currently serving House of Windsor in 1917. Both dynastic names are offshoots of the 800 plus years old House of Wettin.

George, Duke of Brunswick-Luneburg, is considered the first members of the House of Hanover. When the Duchy of Brunswick-Luneburg was divided in 1635, George inherited the principalities of Calenberg and Gottingen, and in 1636 he moved his residence to Hanover. His son, Duke Ernest Augustus, was elevated to price-elector of the Holy Roman Empire in 1692. Ernest Augustus's wife, Sophia of the Palatinate, was declared heiress of the throne of Great Britain (then England and Scotland) by the Act of Settlement 1701, which decreed Roman Catholics could not accede to the throne. Sophia was at the time the nearest Protestant relative to King William III. William himself was actually *of the Dutch House of Orange=Nassau, but both his wife (co-ruler) and mother were Stuart princesses.*

*Ernest Augustus and Sophia's son, George I became the first British monarch of the House of Hanover. The dynasty provided six British monarchs. Of the Kingdoms of Great Britain and Ireland: George I (1714-1727), George II (1727-1760), George III (1760-1820). Of the United Kingdom of Great Britain and Ireland: George III (1760-1820), George IV (1820-1830), William IV (1830-1837), Victoria, (1837-1901). George II, George III, and I also served as electors and dukes of Brunswick-Luneburg, informally, Electors of Hanover. From 1814 when Hanover became a kingdom, the British monarch was also King of Hanover.*

*In 1837, however, the personal union of the thrones of the United Kingdom and Hanover ended. Succession to the Hanoverian throne was regulated by Salic law, which forbade inheritance by a woman, so that is passed not to Queen Victoria but to her uncle, the Duke of Cumberland. In 1901, when Queen Victoria died, the House of Saxe-Coburg and Gotha ascended to the UK throne as her son and heir, Edward VII, as son of her husband, Prince Albert of Saxe-Coburg-Gotha, genealogically belonged to that House-asserting, thereby, that the name of the UK's Royal House changed because of his father was Edward VII's surname.*

*After the death of William IV in 1837 the following kings of Hanover continued the dynasty: Ernest Augustus (1837-1851), George V (1851-1866). The Kingdom of Hanover came to an end in 1866 when it was annexed by Prussia. The 1866 rift between the House of Hanover and the House of Hohenzollern was settled only by the 1913 marriage of Princess Victoria Louise of Prussia to Ernest Augustus, Duke of Brunswick.*

## New Hanover County, North Carolina

*New Hanover County was formed in 1729 as New Hanover Precinct of Bath County, from Craven Precinct. It was named for the House of Hanover, which was the ruling Great Britain. In 1734 parts of New Hanover Precinct became Bladen Precinct and Onslow Precinct. With the abolition of Bath County in 1739, all of its constituent precincts became counties. In 1750 the northern part of New Hanover County became Duplin County. In 1764 another part of New Hanover County was combined with part of Bladen County to form Brunswick County. Finally, in 1875 the separation of northern New Hanover County to form Pender County reduced it to its present dimensions.*

*Some of the closing battles of the American Civil War happened in the county with the Second Battle of Fort Fisher (the last major coastal stronghold of the Confederacy) and the Battle of Wilmington. The Wilmington Insurrection of 1898 and its establishment of Jim Crow laws closed out the 19th-Century with civil rights injustices, which would last until the African-American Civil Rights Movement through the second half of the 20th Century, three generation later. The insurrection was planned by a group of nine conspirators, which included Hugh MacRae. He later donated land to New Hanover County for a park was name for him. In the park still stands a plaque in his honor that does not mention his role in the 1898 insurrection. (25)*

*When speaking of the advancements of New Hanover County over the many years of social and economic problems that face Native Americans and Afro-Americans under Jim Crow it is a proud day in the 21st Century when we can say that we have a Benjamin and Edith Spaulding Descendants Sandra Spaulding Hughes of mix blood ancestry serving Pender and New Hanover Counties, district 18, in the North Carolina House of Representatives. (27)*

*New Hanover County, North Carolina is divided into 5 townships: Cape Fear, Federal Point, Harnett, Masonboro, and its county seat Wilmington. New Hanover is a progressive county and has many tourist attractions, which include Carolina Beach, Kure Beach, Wilmington and Wrightsville Beach.*

*As of the census of 2000 there were 160,307 people residing in the county. The racial makeup of the county was 79.91 % White, 16.97 % African American, .39 % Native American, .83% Asian, .06 % Pacific Islander, .79% from other races, and 1.05% from two or more races, 2.04 % of the population were Hispanic or Latino. (26)*

## *The Establishment of Bladen County, North Carolina*

*Bladen County was formed in 1734 as Bladen Precinct of Bath County, from New Hanover Precinct. It was named for Martin Bladen, a member of the Board of Trade. The territory of Bladen was a vast wilderness with indefinite northern and western boundaries. Reductions in its extent began in 1750, when its western part became Anson County. In 1752 the northern part of Bladen County was combined with parts of Granville county and Johnston County to form Orange County. In 1754 the northern part of what was left of Bladen County became Cumberland County. In 1764 the southern part of what remained of Bladen County was combined with part of New Hanover County to form Brunswick County. In 1787 the western part of the now much smaller county became Robeson. Finally, in 1808 the southern part of Bladen County was combined with part of Brunswick County to form Columbus County.*

*In Bladen County there is a small Native American populations, specifically descendants of the Siouan Indians. Some of the family names that are associated with the Siouan Indians of Bladen County are Blanks, Young's, Moore, Grahams, Spaulding, Campbell, Jacobs, and Mitchell. Land Deeds can be found on many of these families, which show that they were here during Colonial days. These families with Native American ancestry still own mass territory of land today within Bladen County.*

It has been a constant struggle for the Native American people in Bladen County to maintain their identity and not be group with the Afro-American or with Caucasian Population within the county. Presently, the Siouan Indian Tribe in Bladen County has North Carolina State Recognition and is seeking Federal Recognition.

The county is divided into eighteen townships: Abbottsburg, Bethel, Bladenboro, Brown Marsh, Carvers Creek, Central, Clarkton, Colly, Cypress Creek, Elizabethtown, East Arcadia, Frenches Creek, Hollow Lake Creek, Tarheel, Turnbull, White Oak and Whites Creek.

The United State Census Bureau stated that the county has a total area of 887 square miles, of which, 875 square miles of it is land and 12 square miles of it is water. According to the 2000 Census there were 32,278 people living in Bladen County. The racial makeup of the county is 57.22% White, 37.91% African American, 2.04 % Native American, .10% Asian, .04% Pacific Islander, 1.97% from other races, and .73 % from two or more races, 3.7% Hispanic or Latino. (28)

## Columbus County, North Carolina

Columbus County is a county located in the United States of America in the State of North Carolina. The County was formed in 1808 from parts of Bladen County and Brunswick County. The county was named after Christopher Columbus, who was born in 1451 and died on May 20$^{th}$ 1506.

Christopher Columbus whom the county was name after was a Genoese navigator, colonizer and explorer whose voyages across the Atlantic Ocean led to general European awareness of the American continents in the Western Hemisphere. Although not the first to reach the Americas from Europe he was preceded by the Norse, led by Leif Ericson, who built a temporary settlement 500 years earlier at L'Anse aux Meadows. (29) Columbus initiated widespread contact between Europeans and indigenous Americans. With his four voyages of discovery and several attempts at establishing a settlement on the island of Hispaniola, all funded by Queen Isabella of Spain, he initiated the process of Spanish colonization, which foreshadowed general European colonization of the New World. His initial 1492 voyage came at a critical time of growing national imperialism and economic competition between developing nation states seeking wealth from the establishment of trade routes and colonies. In this sociopolitical climate, Columbus far fetched scheme won the attention of Queen Isabella of Spain. Severely underestimating the circumference of the earth, he estimated that a westward route from Iberia to the Indies would be shorter and more direct than the overland trade route through Arabia. If true, this would allow Spain entry into the lucrative spice trade-heretofore commanded by the Arabs and Italians. Following his plotted course, he instead landed within the Bahamas Archipelago at a locale he named San Salvador. Mistaking the North –American island for the East-Asian mainland, he referred to its inhabitants as "Indios". The anniversary of Columbus's 1492 landing in the Americas is observed as Columbus Day on October 12$^{th}$ in Spain and throughout the Americas, except that in the United States it is observed on the second Monday in October.

Surnames such as Campbell, Spaulding, Moore, Mitchell, Blanks, Jacobs, and Grahams were some of the earlier settlers within Columbus and Bladen Counties. These families are primarily located in Bolton, Lake Waccamaw, Brown Marsh, Welch Creek townships. They are predominantly from Native American Descent with traces of Caucasians and Afro-American blood in some of them. Within, Columbus County you have predominantly the Siouan Stock, however, some families are mixed with Cherokee, Tuscarora and Lumbee Indians, and there are some of the Spaulding Descendants mix with Lumbee, Siouan, Cherokee, and Tuscarora Indians . First, there are Indian Census records of George Spaulding (1856) son of Benjamin Spaulding Jr. son of Benjamin Spaulding (1773-1862). Secondly, Elsie Chavis Blanks who moved to Columbus County and married Joshua Blanks was from Pembroke, North Carolina and was a Tuscarora Indian. (31)

*Many of the present day Native American within the county still are landowners. The Native American Indian can still be found living in present day Columbus County. (32) It is amazing within Columbus County that you still have small remnant tribes of Native People living their despite order to exterminate and move all Indian west of the Mississippi by President Andrew Jackson.*

*Columbus County, North Carolina has seven incorporated towns: Bolton, Cerro Gordo, Chadbourn, Fair Bluff, Tabor City, Lake Waccamaw, and Whiteville which is the county seat. Also, there are nine townships: Bogue, Bug Hill, Lees, Ransom, South Williams, Taturns, Welch Creek, Western Prong and Williams.*

Rev. Robert Owen Spaulding Estate,
located in Columbus County,
North Carolina built in 1872

*According to the 2000 Census report there were 54,749 people residing in Columbus County. The racial makeup for the county was 64.9 % White, 31.1% African American, 3.1 % Native American, .2% Asians, 2.7% from other races, and .6% from two or more races, 2.7% of the population were Hispanic or Latino. (30)*

## Brunswick County, North Carolina

*Brunswick County was formed in 1764 from parts of Bladen County and New Hanover County. It was named for the colonial port of Brunswick town (now in ruins), which was itself named for Duchy of Brunswick-Luneburg; at the time held by the British kings of the House of Hanover. ) Brunswick County is a county with many beautiful beaches and also it is becoming one of North Carolina major retirement center. The small Native American presence in the county are remnants of the Lake Waccamaw Siouan Tribe and surnames such as Campbell, Graham, Jacobs, Blanks, and Mitchell are among the Native American Population.*

*The county is divided into six townships: Lockwoods Folloy, Northwest, Shallotte, Smithville Township, Town Creek, and Waccamaw. Brunswick County consist of the following cities and towns: Bald Head Island, Belville, Boiling Spring Lakes, Bolivia, Calabash, Carolina Shores, Caswell Beach, Holden Beach, Leland, Navassa, Northwest, Oak Island, Ocean Isle Beach, Sandy Creek, Shallotte, Southport, St James, Sunset Beach, Varnamtown.*

*In the 2000 Census of the United States there were 73,143 people residing in the county. The racial makeup of the county was 82.3 % white, 14.38 % African American, .68 % Native American, .27% Asian, .04 Pacific Islander, 1.32 % from other races, and 1.01 % from two or more races, 2.68 % of the population were Hispanic or Latino. (33).*

*Milton E. Campbell*

## Robeson County, North Carolina

*Robeson County was incorporated in 1787 from Bladen County, and was named in honor of Col. Thomas Robeson of Tar Heel, North Carolina for his Revolutionary War Service. While Col. Robeson never lived in the county that now bears his name, toward the end of the war in 1781, he and 70 colonial rebels defeated an army of 400 loyalists at the Battle of Elizabethtown. The county seat of Robeson County is Lumberton, which is a progressive city in the state of North Carolina. (34) Robeson County is bounded by the state of South Carolina, and the North Carolina counties of Bladen, Columbus, Cumberland, Hoke, and Scotland. Municipalities and communities are the city of Lumberton and towns are Fairmont, Lumber, Bridge, Marietta, Maxton, McDonald, Orrum, Parkton, Pembroke, Proctorville, Raynham, Red Springs, Rennert, Rowland, and St. Pauls. Townships within the county are Maxton, Barker Ten Mile, Elrod, Prospect, Raemon, Rex, and Shannon.*

*The Lumbee Indian Tribe of North Carolina are located in Robeson County and comprises more than one-half the state of North Carolina indigenous population of 84,000. With a population of 58,443, reflecting a 34.5 % increase from the 1980 populations of 43,465 members. The Lumbee reside primarily in Robeson, Hoke, Cumberland, and Scotland counties. In Robeson County alone, there are currently 46,869 Lumbee Indians out of a total county population of 123,339, and thus the Lumbee make up 38.02%, making them the largest racial/ethnic group in the county. In fact, the Lumbee are also the largest tribal nation east of the Mississippi River, the ninth largest tribal nation, and the largest non-reservation tribe of Native Americans in the United States. (36)*

*Archaeological excavation performed in Robeson County reveals a long and rich history of widespread and consistent occupation of the region, most especially near the Lumber River since the end of the last Ice Age. Local excavations indicate that Native American peoples made stone tools using materials brought into present-day Robeson County from* the Carolina Piedmont. The large amounts of ancient pottery found at some Robeson County sites have been dated to the early Woodland period, and suggest that Native American settlements around the river were part of an extensive trade network with other regions. If anything, portions of the river basin show that Robeson County was a "zone of cultural interactions. (37,38)" After colonial contact, European-made items, such as kaolin tobacco pipes, were traded by the Spanish, French, and the English to Native American peoples of the coast, and found their way to the Robeson County region long before Europeans established permanent settlements along the Lumber River.

Swamps, streams, and artesian wells provided an excellent supply of water for Native people. Fish was plentiful, and the regions lush vegetation included numerous food crops. "Carolina bays" continue to dot the landscape, and if the sheer number of 10,000-year-old Clovis points found along their banks are any indication, Native peoples found these unique depressions filled with water to be ideal campsites.

## Colonial Incursions

Early written sources specific to the Robeson County region are few for the post-contact period of European colonization. Surveyors for the Wineau factory charted a village of Waccamaw Indians on the Lumber River, a few miles west of the present-day town of Pembroke, North Carolina on a map in 1725. In 1754, North Carolina Governor Arthur Dobbs received a report from his agent, Col. Rutherford, the head of Bladen County militia that a "mix crew" of 50 Indian families was living along Drowning Creek. The communication also reported the shooting of a surveyor who entered the area" to view vacant lands." These are the first written account of the Native peoples from whom the Lumbee descend.

Bladen County encompassed a portion of what is today Robeson County, and the Lumber River was at this time called by English colonials, "Drowning Creek." After the violent upheavals of the Yamasee War of

*Milton E. Campbell*

*1715-1717, and the Tuscarora War of 1711-1715. Families of Waccamaw Indians had left South Carolina Colony in 1718, and established a village west of present-day Pembroke, North Carolina by 1725. The "mixed crew" that Rutherford observed in 1754 were located in the same locale as the earlier Waccamaw settlement.*

*The research of the noted anthropologist, John R. Swanton of the Smithsonian Institution collaborates much of the oral tradition of the Lumbee Indians of Robeson County. Swanton posited that the Lumbee were the descendants of Siouan peoples of which the most prominent were the Cheraw and Keyauwee. (37.38) These communities that would later comprise the Lumbee would also have included Siouan refugee groups of the eno, Shakori, as well as coastal groups such as the Waccamaw and Cape Fear Indians. Colonial migrants to the present-day Robeson County Lumber River basin came into contact with an acculturated population of Native Americans who reportedly spoke some English, owned European trade goods, and used primitive English-style farm tools in their agricultural pursuits. (39) By then, English Gaelic speaking highland Scots, and Welsh colonials had begun to make their way from present-day Fayetteville, North Carolina, to Laurinburg, North Carolina, and eventually, to Drowning Creek, or the present-day Lumber River. Critical to keep in mind is that at the same time that Native peoples were fleeing into the Robeson County region and seeking refuge from the incalculable destruction of warfare and disease, European colonials were in pursuit, attempting to gain a foothold, then wrest control of the region of Robeson County.*

*By the mid-eighteenth century, Indians continued to populate the Lumber River basin area and its numerous tributaries. Whites slowly moved into and established settlements, but overall, they initially lived on the periphery of those lands to which the ancestors of the Lumbee had managed to secure title with the colonial administration of North Carolina. The main Indian settlements during the late eighteenth century were Prospect and Red Banks. (40) Individual land ownership by Native Americans had far-reaching consequences for the history of Robeson County in that Native peoples were less subject to the political* and economic dominance of whites, managing to live in a homogeneous network of settlements that provided social and cultural security.

By the middle of the nineteenth century however, settlement patterns had shifted: now ancestral Lumbee settlements were interspersed among faster growing white communities, and the name of the region's river was changed again. A lottery was used to dispose of lots with which to establish Lumberton. The town was later incorporated in 1788, and John Willis proposed the name "Lumberton" for the site, the name of which derives from the Lumber River, or is a reference to the lumber and naval stores industry that began to dominate, and continued to dominate the economy of Robeson County throughout the nineteenth century. The section of the Lumber River where Lumberton is located was known throughout that century as "Drowning Creek" was renamed the Lumber River.

The first Robeson County courthouse was erected on land, which formed a part of the "Red Bluff Plantation", owned by Lumberton founder, John Willis. Robeson County post office was established in 1794, and much like today, from the end of the eighteenth- to the mid-nineteenth centuries, numerous languages could be hear throughout Robeson County: the Gaelic of the highland Scots and the Welsh, English, and one can speculate, remnant Siouan, Algonquian, and Iroquoian languages of the ancestral Lumbee.

By the beginning of the American Civil War, most Native Americans attempted to eke out an impoverished existence. Their status had continued to decline. Since 1790, Native Americans in the southern states were enumerated as "free persons of color" on the local and federal census. By 1835, and in the wake of the convergence of three historical events. Nat Turner's Rebellion, the ratification of the North Carolina Constitutional Convention, and Indian removal, they were summarily stripped of their previously held right to vote, serve on juries, own and use firearms, and to learn to read and write. The gradual dispossession of tribal lands accelerated, and Robeson County Native Americans regarded the local white slave-owning elite as robbers and oppressors.

*Milton E. Campbell*

*With the establishment of Croatan Norman School on March 7, 1887, it was the beginning of a socially, economically and educational opportunities for the county. In 1939 it became a four-year institution, a change followed in 1941 by a new name: Pembroke State College for Indians. A change of name to Pembroke State College in 1949 presaged the admission of white students, which was approved in 1950. Brown v. Board of Education decision in 1954 eliminated all race restrictions. (41) In 1969 the college became Pembroke State University, a regional university that was incorporated into the University of North Carolina system in 1972. This University provides great opportunities for the Native American population and other ethic groups within the state and country.*

*In the present day 21$^h$ Century Robeson County has continue to advance socially, economically and educational with the establishment of The University of North Carolina at Pembroke.*

*The 2000 Census of the United States of America list 123,339 inhabitants residing in the county. The racial makeup of the county was 38.02% Native American, 32.8% White, 25.11% African American, 4.85 % Hispanic or Latino, .33% Asian, .06% Pacific Islander, 2.26% from other races, 1.41% from two or more races. (35)*

## Cumberland County, North Carolina

Cumberland County was formed in 1754 from Bladen County. The county was named for Prince William Augustus, Duke of Cumberland (1721-1765), captain-general of the British army and victorious commander at the Battle of Culloden. In 1771 parts of Cumberland County, Johnston County, and Orange County were combined to form Wake County. In July 1784 the western part of Cumberland County became Moore County; the eastern part became Fayette County in honor of the Marquis de la Fayette, but the name Cumberland County was restored three months later. In 1855 the northern part of Cumberland County became Harnett County. Finally, in 1911 parts of Cumberland County and Robeson County were combined to form Hoke County.

It must be stated that Cumberland County is home to Fayetteville State University, which historical is a predominant Afro-American Institution. Many Benjamin and Edith Jacobs Spaulding Descendants attended this University and made major contribution toward the advancement of Fayetteville State University. Specially speaking, Dr. Charles Clinton Spaulding and Mrs. Agnes Spaulding Hill made major donations during the 20th Century.

The present day Cumberland County is divided into eleven townships: Beaver Dam, Black River, Carvers Creek, Cedar Creek, Cross Creek, Eastover, Gray's Creek, Manchester, Pearce's Mill, Rockfish, and Seventy-First.

The county seat is Fayetteville and the 2000 census states that there were 302, 963 residents in the county. By 2005 the racial makeup of the county was 51.5 % non-Hispanic whites, 36.7 % African American, 6.4% Latino, 3.1% of the population reported more than one race, 2.1% of the population was Asian and 1.7% of the population was Native American. (42)

*Milton E. Campbell*

## Orange County, North Carolina

Orange County was formed in 1752 from parts of Bladen County, Granville County, and Johnston County. It was named for the infant William V of Orange, whose mother Anne, daughter of King George II of Great Britain, was then regent of the Dutch Republic. In 1771, Orange County was reduced in area and the western part of it was combined with the eastern part of Rowan County to form Guilford County. Another part was combined with parts of Cumberland County and Johnston County to form Wake County. The southern part of what remained became Chatham County. In 1777, the northern half of what was left of Orange County became Caswell County. In 1849 the western third of the still shrinking county became Alamance County. Finally, in 1881 the eastern half of the county's remaining territory was combined with part of Wake County to form Durham County. Some of the first settlers of the county were English Quakers, who settled along the Haw and Eno Rivers. (43) Arguably, the earliest settlers in the county were the Andrews Family, which would later marry into the Lloyd family. (44)

## Colonial Period and Revolutionary War

The county seat of Orange County is the city of Hillsborough, which was founded in 1754, and was first owned, surveyed, and mapped by William Churton (a surveyor for Earl Granville). Originally to be named Orange, it was named Corbin Town (for Francis Corbin, a member of the governor's council and one of Granville's land agents) in 1759. It was not until 1766 that it was named Hillsborough, after Earl of Hillsborough, the British secretary of state for the colonies and a relative of royal Governor William Tryon.

Hillsborough was an earlier Piedmont colonial town where court was held, and was the scene of some pre-Revolutionary War tensions. In the late 1760s, tension between Piedmont farmers and coastal planters welled up in the *Regulator movement*, which had its epicenter in *Hillsborough (45)*. Several thousand people from North Carolina, mainly from Orange County, Anson County, and Granville County in the western region, were extremely dissatisfied with the wealthy North Carolina officials whom they considered cruel, arbitrary, tyrannical and corrupt. Many inland farmers found themselves unable to pay their taxes and resented the consequent seizure of their property. Local sheriffs sometime kept taxes for their own gain and sometimes charged twice for the same tax. At times, sheriffs would intentionally remove records of their tax collection in order to further tax citizens. The most heavily affected areas were said to be that of Rowan, Anson, Orange, Granville, and Cumberland counties. It was a struggle of mostly lower class citizens, who made up the majority of the population of North Carolina, and the wealthy ruling class, who composed about 5 % of the population, yet maintained almost total control of the government. It is estimated that out of the 8,000 people living in Orange County at the time, some six or seven thousand of them were in support of the Regulators.

Governor William Tryon's conspicuous consumption in the construction of a new governor's mansion at New Bern fuelled the movement's resentment. As the western districts were districts were under-represented in the colonial legislature, it was difficult for the farmers to obtain redress by legislative means. Ultimately, the frustrated farmers took to arms and closed the court in Hillsborough; dragging those they saw as corrupt officials through the streets and cracking the church bell. (45) Tryon sent troops from his militia to the region and defeated the Regulators at the Battle of Alamance in May 1771. (45) Several trails were held after the war, resulting in the hanging of six Regulators at Hillsborough on June 19$^{th}$, 1771.

Hillsborough was used as the home of the North Carolina state legislature during the American Revolution. (46) Hillsborough served as a military base by British General Charles Cornwallis in 1781. The United States Constitution drafted in 1787 was controversial in North Carolina. Delegate meetings at Hillsboro in July 1788 initially voted to reject it for anti-federalist reasons. They were persuaded to change their minds partly by the strenuous efforts of James Iredell and William Davies and partly by the protest of a Bill of rights. The Constitution was later ratified by North Carolina at a convention in Fayetteville.

## Duplin County

Duplin County is a county located in North Carolina. The county was formed in 1750 from New Hanover County. It was named for Thomas Hay, Viscount Duplin, and later 9th Earl of Kinnoull. In 1784 the western part of Duplin County became Sampson County. One of Duplin's favorite sons, John Miller, was postmaster and merchant in Duplin. He migrated to Leon County, Florida, with other North Carolinians between 1830 and 1840 and established a successful plantation called Miccosukee Plantation.

The county is divided into thirteen townships: Albertson, Cypress Creek, Faison, Glisson, Island Creek, Kenansville, Limestone, Magnolia, Rockfish, Rose Hill, Smith, Warsaw, and Wolfscrape.

Present day Duplin County is important in raising animals for food. It has more swine than any other county in the United States. The county is also the home to a major chicken and turkey industry. (47) Within the last few years it has been Duplin County has developed in to a wine making county with the opening of the Duplin County Winery.

As of the census of 2000, there were 49,063 people residing in the county. The racial makeup of the county was 58.67% white, 28.94 % African American, .23% Native American, .15% Asian, .07% Pacific Islander, 10.87 % from other races, and 1.06% from two or more races, 15.14 % of the population were Hispanic or Latino. (42)

## Anson County

*Anson County was formed in 1750 from Bladen County. It was named for George Anson, Baron Anson, a British admiral, who circumnavigated the globe from 1740 to 1744, and later became First Lord of Admiralty. Like its parent county Bladen, Anson County was originally a vast territory with indefinite northern and western boundaries. Reductions in its extent began in 1753, when the northern part of it became Rowan County. In 1762 the western part of Anson County became Mecklenburg County. In 1779 the northern part of what remained of Anson County became Montgomery County, and the part east of the Pee Dee River became Richmond County. Finally, in 1842 the western part of Anson County was combined with the southeastern part of Mecklenburg County to become Union County.*

*Anson County is noted for filmmaking, especially, Steven Spielberg filmed The Color Purple mostly in Wadesboro, and a large white farmhouse (the Hautley house, which is located in Lileville, North Carolina and is an old farmhouse located few miles off Highway 74) was used extensively as the main exterior location in that film. Most of the town scenes were done in nearly by Marshville, North Carolina in Union County. Marshville is a small town in the county directly to the west of Anson County: the store is an actual store called Apple Jacks and dirt was laid out of over pavement during filming. The film Evil Dead II was also filmed in Wadesboro, and the Hautley house became the production office for the film. Most of the Evil Dead II was shot in the woods near that farmhouse, or J.R. Junior High School, which is where the interior cabin set, was located. Also within present day Anson County the Pee Dee National Wildlife Refuge can be found.*

*As of the census of 2000, there were 25,275 people residing in the county. The racial makeup of the county was 49.53% White, 48.64 African American, .45% Native American, .57% Asian, .02% Pacific Islander, .32% from other races, and .46% from two or more races, .83% of the population were Hispanic or Latino. (42)*

# CHAPTER III

## History of American Indians living in the interior of the American Southwest

In describing the history of the American Indians living in the interior of the American southwest, scholars use the term prehistory for the time before 1492 and 1540, European contact. This was the period when the Spanish under Hernando de Soto first passed through Cherokee country. De Soto's expedition visited many of the Georgia and Tennessee villages later identified as Cherokee, but recorded them as then ruled by the Coosa chiefdom. To the northeast, the Chiska inhabited all the country surrounding Whitetop Mountain where Tennessee, Virginia, and North Carolina meet, while a Chalaque nation was recorded as living around the Keowee River where North Carolina, South Carolina and Georgia meet.(48)

Under Juan Pardo, Spanish troops built a total of six forts in 1567 in the interior: at the regional chiefdom of Joara and other towns in 1567-68. It was part of a path he was trying to fortify to go west to Spanish silver mining settlements in Mexico. Joara was a chiefdom of the Mississippian mound builder culture, established about 1000 A.D. The Spanish alienated the natives over the months and were soon destroyed. (49)

Failed attempts at colonization, Europeans had no recorded contact with Indians in the southeast for nearly a century. The term protohistory is sometimes used for this period. What happened during this time is uncertain, but the territory of the former Coosa and Chiska Nations seems to have been dominated by the Cherokee. The members of the former groups were either assimilated by the larger Cherokee nation, *or altered the names of their tribes and moved elsewhere. Since historic documentation is generally lacking, Cherokee prehistory and protohistory have been studied via oral tradition, linguistic analysis, and archaeology.*

*North Carolina has the highest American Indian population of states on the East Coast. The estimated population figures for Native Americans in North Carolina as of 2004 were 110,198. To date, North Carolina recognizes eight Native American tribal nations within it state borders. Those tribes are the Coharie, Eastern Band of the Cherokee, Haliwa-Saponi, Lumbee, Mehrrin, Sappony, Occaneechi Band of the Saponi Nation and Waccamaw-Siouan.*

# Chapter IV

## *Coharie Indians Tribe who descend from the Neusiok Indians*

The Coharie are a Native American Tribe who descend from the Neusiok Indians on the Little Coharie River, in Sampson and Harnett County, North Carolina. The Coharie are one of eight state recognized Native American tribes in North Carolina. The Coharie have intermarried predominantly with the Lumbee and Tuscarora Indians of Robeson County, as well as with the Eastern Band of Cherokee Indians.

## *History of the Coharie Indians*

Historians generally contend that the Coharie descendants of the Newusiok, Coree, Tuscarora, and Waccamaw, who occupied what is now the central portion of North Carolina. In the early seventeenth century, the Coree was ensconced along the Big Coharie and Little Coharie rivers in present-day Sampson County. Between 1730 and 1745, intertribal conflicts as well as hostilities between Native peoples and English colonials turned the Southeast, and in particular, the Carolinas into a maelstrom of violent activity from the acceleration of the Deerskin and Indian Slave trades, to the spread of disease and disruptions of warfare. Families of Coree, Waccamaw, and Neusiok Indians began to seek refuge from colonial incursions in northern and northeastern North Carolina and moved into what is now Harnett and Sampson counties. During, the 1800s, the Coharie built their political base in Sampson County. They held the right to own and use firearms, and vote in local elections. However, with the convergence of Indian removal policy on the federal level, and the ratification of the 1835 amendment to North Carolina's constitution on the state level, the Coharie, much like their Native and free black neighbors, found themselves politically vulnerable. In 1835, the state of North Carolina disenfranchised the Coharie (50).

Nevertheless, in 1859, the Coharie established their own subscription school. In 1911, the Coharie asked North Carolina to provide Indian schools in Sampson County. In the same year, the Coharie established New Bethel Indian School in New Bethel Township, Sampson County. In 1912, the Coharie established a school in Herring Township, after the first year of which, the state stopped supporting the school. (51) Following the precedent set by the Lumbee Indians of Robeson County, the Coharie established a semi-independent school system where in North Carolina retained some oversight. While the state legislature rescinded its permission in 1913, it reinstated the separate Coharie school system four years later given the activism of the tribe and the assistance of its tribal attorney. In 1917, the East Carolina Indian School was built in Herring Township, and in 1942, East Carolina Indian School was established in Sampson County.

## Demographics

The Coharie Indian population of Harnett and Sampson counties has steadily increased from 755 in 1970 to 2,700 in 2007. The tribe consist predominantly adults between the ages of 21-65. According to the 2000 census of the United States, the Coharie tribe consists of 2,632 enrolled members, and approximately 20% reside outside of the tribal communities in Harnett and Sampson counties. The four settlements recognized by the Coharie Indian tribal Council is Holly Grove, New Bethel, Shiloh, and Antioch.

In 1971, the state of North Carolina recognized the Coharie Tribe and Clinton, North Carolina is the tribal seat. In 1975, the tribe chartered the Coharie Intra-Tribal Council to serve as a private non-

*profit organization established to promote the health, education, social and economic well being of the Native people of Sampson and Harnett Counties. The Coharie Intra-Tribal Council is housed in the old Eastern Carolina Indian School building, a school that served the Native Americans of Sampson, Harnett, Cumberland, Columbus, Person, and Hoke counties from 1942 until 1966. The Coharie Indian Tribe elected their first tribal chief in 1910. A tribal chief and seven tribal council members lead tribal affairs. The Coharie political leadership oversees the four communities of Coharie Indians from three geographical locations in Sampson County and one region in Harnett County.*

Coharie Indian Chief

# Chapter V

## *Cherokee Indian from the Southern United States*

The Cherokee are a Native American people from the Southern United States. They are located principally in Georgia, the Carolinas and Eastern Tennessee. Linguistically, they are connected to speakers of the Iroquoian language family. The Cherokees were known as one of the "Five Civilized Tribes", in the 19th century because they had assimilated numerous cultural and technological practices of their European-American neighbors. The 2000 Census of the United States identify the Cherokee Indians as the largest of the 563 federally recognized Native American tribes in the United States. (52)

The Cherokee refer to themselves as Tsalagi or Aniyvwiyai, which means "Principal People". The Iroquois called the Cherokee Oyata'ge'ronon which means inhabitants of the cave country. Many theories about the orgin of the word Cherokee exist. It may have originally been derived from the Choctwa word Cha-la-kee, which means those who live in the mountains. (53) The earliest Spanish spelling of Cherokee, from 1755, is "Tchalaquei". (54) Another theory is Cherokee derives from a Muscogee Creek word, meaning "those that live by Cherry Creek".

## *Cherokee Origins*

Native Americans or Paleo-Indian appeared in what is today the Southern United States over 14,000 years ago. (55) Paleo-Indians in the Southeast were hunter-gatherers who pursued a wide range of animals, including the megafauna, which became extinct following the end of the

*Pleistocene age. (55)* It is commonly assumed that Paleo-Indians were specialized, highly mobile foragers that hunted late Pleistocene fauna such as bison antiques, mastodons, caribou, and mammoths, although direct evidence is meager in the Southeast.(55)

During the Archaic Period, the Cherokees began to cultivate plants such as marsh elder, lambsquarters, sunflowers, pigweed, and some native squash. During Mississippian Period (900A.D. to 1500 A.D.), Cherokee ancestors developed a new variety of corn called eastern flint, which closely resembles modern corn. Also, the Green Corn Ceremony was held during this period and families, clans, and tribes came together for prayers, dances, marriages, and reconciliations.

Much of what is known about pre-19th century Cherokee culture and society comes from the papers of American writer John Howard Payne. The Payne papers describe the account by Cherokee elders of a traditional societal structure in which a group referred to as the "White Organization" of leaders represented the seven clans. This group which was hereditary and described as priestly, was responsible for religious activities such as healing, purification, and prayer. A second group of younger men, the "red organization", was responsible for warfare. Warfare was considered a polluting activity, which required the purification of the priestly class before participants could reintegrate into normal village life.(56)

James Mooney, who studied the Cherokee in the late 1880's, first traced the decline of the former hierarchy.(57) Mooney observed the structure of Cherokee religious practitioners was more informal, base more on individual knowledge and ability than upon heredity. In addition, separation of the Eastern Cherokee, who had not been subject to the Indian removal and remained in the mountains of western North Carolina, further complicated the traditional hierarchies.(56)

Unlike most other Indian in the American southeast at the start of the historic era, the Cherokee spoke an Iroquoian language. (Other exceptions were the Tuscarora, Nottoway, Meherrin, and Coree.) Since the region east of the Great Lakes was the core of Iroquoian language speakers, scholars have theorized that the Cherokee migrated south from that region. However, others believe that the Iroquois migrated north from the southeast, with the Tuscarora braking off from that group during the migration. Linguistic analysis shows a relatively large difference between Cherokee and the northern Iroquoian languages, indicating a split in the distant past. (58) Glottochronology studies suggest the split occurred between about 1,500 and 1,800 B.C.(59) The ancient settlement of Kituwa on the Tuckasegee River, formerly next to and now part of Qualla Boundary ( the reservation of the Eastern Band of Cherokee Indians), is often cited as the original Cherokee settlement in the Southeast.(58)

## English contact with the Cherokee Indians of North America

James Mooney documents indicate that the English first had contact with the Cherokee in 1654. Around this time, a tribe they knew from the west and settled near the falls of the James River threatened the Powhatan. While some scholars have linked these references to the Cherokee, others deduce they were a Siouan tribe, since they appeared in company with Monacan and Nahyssan groups.

An expedition by James Needham and Gabriel Arthur, sent in 1673 by fur-trader Abraham Wood from Fort Henry which is modern day Petersburg, Virginia, to the Overhill Cherokee country. Wood hoped to forge a direct trading connection with the Cherokee to bypass the Occaneechi Indians, who were serving as middlemen on the Trading Path. Two colonial Virginians did make contact with the Cherokee. Needham departed with a guide nickname 'Indian John' while Arthur was left behind to learn the Cherokee language. During the journey, Needham engaged in an argument with Indian John which resulted in his death. Indian John then tried to encourage his tribe to kill Arthur but the chief prevented this. Arthur, disguised as a Cherokee, accompanied the chief of the Cherokee tribe at Chota on raids of

*Spanish settlements in Florida, Indian communities on the east coast, and Shawnee towns on the Ohio River. However, in 1674, the Shawnee Indians who discovered that under his disguise of clay and ash he was a white man captured him. The Shawnee did not kill Arthur but alternatively allowed him to return to Chota. In June of 1674, the chief escorted Arthur back to his English settlement in Virginia. By the late seventeenth century, colonial traders from both Virginia and South Carolina were making regular journeys to Cherokee lands, but few wrote about their experiences.*

*The events of the early trading contact period have been pieced together by historian's examination of records of colonial laws and lawsuits involving traders. The trade was mainly deerskins, raw material for the booming European leather industry, in exchange for European technology "trade goods", such as iron and steel tools, firearms, gunpowder, and ammunition. By 1705, traders complained that their business has been lost and replaced by Indian slave trade instigated by Governor James Moore of South Carolina. Moore had commissioned people to" set upon, assault, kill, destroy, and take captive as many Indians as possible". When the captives were sold, traders split profits with the Governor. (60) Although colonial governments early prohibited selling alcohol to Indians, traders commonly used rum and whiskey as common items of trade.(61)*

*Of the southeastern Indian confederacies of the late seventeenth and early eighteenth centuries (Creek, Chickasaw, Choctwaw, etc), the Cherokee were one of the most populous and powerful. They were relatively isolated by their hilly and mountainous homeland. A small-scale trading system was established with Virginia in the late seventeenth century. In 1690s, the Cherokee had founded a much stronger and important trade relationship with the colony of South Carolina, based in Charles Town. By the 1700s, this overshadowed the Virginia relationship.(62)*

## History of the Cherokee Indians during the 18$^{th}$ and 19$^{th}$ Century

The Cherokees gave sanctuary to a band of Shawnee in the 1660s, but from 1710 to 1715 the Cherokee and Chickasaw, allied with the British, fought Shawnee, who were allied with the French, and forced them to move north. Cherokees fought with the Yamasee, Catawba, and British in late 1712 and early 1713 against the Tuscarora in the Second Tuscarora War. The Tuscarora War marked the beginning of an English-Cherokee relationship that, despite breaking down on occasion, remained strong for much of the 18$^{th}$ century.

In January, 1716, a delegation of Muscogee Creek leaders was murdered at the Cherokee town of Tugaloo, marking the Cherokee's entry into the Yamasee War, which ended in 1717 with peace treaties between South Carolina and the Creeks. Hostility and sporadic raids between the Cherokee and Creek continued for decades. (63) These raids came to a head at the Battle of Taliwa in 1755, present-day Ball Ground, Georgia, with the defeat of the Muscogee.

In 1721, the Cherokee ceded lands in South Carolina. In 1730, at Nikwasi, a manipulative Britain, Sir Alexander Cumming convinced Cherokees to crown Moytoy of Tellico as "Emperor." Moytoy agreed to recognize King George II of Great Britain as the Cherokee protector. Seven prominent Cherokee, including Attakullakulla, traveled with Sir Alexander Cuming back to London, England. The Cherokee delegation signed treaty the Treaty of Whitehall with the British. Moytoy's son, Amo-sgasite(Dreadful Water) attempted to succeed him as "Emperor" in 1741, but the Cherokees elected their own leader, Standing Turkey of Echota.(64)

Political Power among Cherokees remained decentralized and towns acting autonomously. In 1735 the Cherokee were estimated to have sixty-four towns and villages and 6000 fighting men. In 1738 and 1739 smallpox epidemics broke out among the Cherokee, who had no natural immunity. Nearly half their population died within a year.

Hundreds of other Cherokee committed suicide due to disfigurement from the disease.

From 1753 to 1755, battles broke out between the Cherokee and Muscogee over disputing hunting grounds in North Georgia. Cherokees were victorious in the Battle of Taliwa. British soldier built forts in Cherokee country to confront the French, including Fort Loudoun near Chota. In 1756 the Cherokees fought with the British in the French and Indian War; however, serious misunderstandings between the two allies arose quickly, resulting in the 1760 Anglo-Cherokee War. A Royal Proclamation of 1763 from King George III forbade British settlements west of the Appalachian crest, attempting to afford some temporary protection from encroachment to the Cherokee, but it proved difficult to enforce.(65)

In 1771-1772, North Carolinian settlers squatted on Cherokee lands in Tennessee, forming the Watauga Association.(66) In Kentucky, Daniel Boone and his party tried to settle in Kentucky, but the Shawnee, Delaware, Mingo, and some Cherokee attacked a scouting and forage party that included Boone's son. This sparked the beginning of what was known as Dumore's War(1773-1774).

In 1776, allied with the Shawnee, led by Cornstalk, Cherokees attacked settlers in South Carolina, Georgia, Virginia, and North Carolina in the Second Cherokee War. Overhill Cherokee Nancy Ward, Dragging Canoe's niece, warned settlers of impending attacks. European-American militias retaliated and destroyed over 50 Cherokee towns. In 1777 surviving Cherokee town leaders signed the treaties with the states.

Dragging Canoe and his band moved near Chattanooga, Tennessee, establishing 11 new towns, Chickamauga was his headquarters and his entire band was known as the Chickamaugas. From here he fought a guerrilla war, the Chickamauga Wars (1776-1794). The Treaty of Tellico Blockhouse, signed on 7th of November 1794, ended the Chickamauga wars.

*During the 19th Century the Cherokees organized a national government of Cherokee led by Principal Chiefs Little Turkey(1788-1801), Black Fox (1801-1811), and Pathkiller (1811-1827). The seat of the Upper Towns was at Ustanali near Calhoun, Georgia, also the titular seat of the Nation, and with the former warriors James Vann and his protégés The Riga (formerly known as PathKiller) and Charles R. Hicks, the "Cherokee Triumvirate", as their dominant leaders, particularly of the younger more acculturated generation. The leaders of these towns were the most progressive, favoring acculturation, formal education, and modern methods of farming. Facing removal, the Lower Cherokee were the first to move west. Remaining Lower Town Leaders, such s Young Dragging Canoe and Swquoyah, were strong advocates of voluntary relocation.*

*Milton E. Campbell*

## Removal Era of the Cherokee Indians

The United States government established a Cherokee Reservation in Arkansas in 1815(67). The reservation boundaries extended from north of the Arkansas River to the southern bank of the White River. The Bowl, Swquoyah, Spring Frog and Tatsi(Dutch) and their bands settled there. These Cherokees became known as "Old Settlers." John Ross became the Principal Chief of the tribe in 1828 and remained the chief until his death in 1866. John Ross led the battle to halt their removal. Ross supporters, commonly referred to as the "National Party." Were opposed by a group known as the "Ridge Party" or the " Treaty Party". The Treaty Party signed the Treaty of New Echota, stipulating terms and conditions for the removal of the Cherokee Nation from the lands in the East for lands in Indian Territory.

## Trail of Tears

The Cherokees were displaced from their ancestral lands in northern Georgia and the Carolinas in a period of rapidly expanding white population. Some of the rapid expansion was due to a gold rush around Dahlonega, Georgia in the 1830s. President Andrew Jackson said removal policy was an effort to prevent the Cherokee from facing the fate of "the Mohegan, the Narragansett, and the Delaware." However there is ample evidence that the Cherokee were adapting modern farming techniques, and modern analysis shown that the area was in general in a state of economic surplus.(67)

The Cherokee were to bring their grievances to US judicial review that set a precedent in Indian Country. In June 1830, a delegation of Cherokee led by Chief Ross defended Cherokee rights before the United States Supreme Court in the Cherokee Nation versus Georgia case. In the case Worcester verse Georgia, the United States Supreme Court held that Cherokee Native Americans were entitled to federal protection from the actions of state governments, which would infringe on the tribe's sovereignty. Worcester verse Georgia is considered one of the most important decisions in law dealing with Native Americans.

Despite the Worcester v. Georgia ruling in their favor, the majority of Cherokees were forcibly relocated westward to Indian Territory in 1838-1839, a migration known as the Trail of Tears or in Cherokee Nvna Duala Tsvyi( The Trail Where They Cried). This took place during the Indian Removal Act of 1830. The harsh treatment the Cherokee received at the hands of white settlers caused some to enroll to emigrate west(68). As some Cherokees were slaveholders, they took enslaved African-Americans with them west of the Mississippi. Intermarried European-Americans and missionaries also walked the Trail of Tears.

On June 22, 1839, Major Ridge and Elias Boundinot were assassinated by a party of twenty-five extremist Ross supporters that included Daniel Colston, John Vann, Archibald Spear, James Spear, Joseph Spear, Hunter, and others. Stand Watie fought off the attempt on his life that day and escaped to
Arkansas.

## Cherokee Freedmen

The Cherokee freedmen, descendants of African American slaves owned by citizens of the Cherokee Nation during the Antebellum Period, were first guaranteed Cherokee citizenship under a treaty with the United States in 1866. This was the wake of the American Civil War, when the US emancipated citizenship in the United States.
In 1988, the federal court in the Freedmen of Nero v. Cherokee Nation held that Cherokees could decide citizenship requirements and exclude freedmen. On March 7, 2006, the Cherokee Nation Judicial Appeal Tribunal ruled that the Cherokee Freedmen were eligible for Cherokee citizenship. This ruling proved controversial; while the Cherokee Freedman had historically been recorded as "citizens" of the Cherokee nation at least since 1866 and the later Dawes Commission Land Rolls, the ruling "did not limit membership to people possessing Cherokee

blood.(69) This ruling was consistent with the 1975 Constitution of the Cherokee Nation of Oklahoma, in its acceptance of the Cherokee Freedmen on the basis of historical citizenship, rather than documented blood relation.

## Modern Cherokee Tribes

During 1898-1906 the federal government dissolved the former Cherokee Nation, to make way for the incorporation of Indian Territory into the new state of Oklahoma. From 1906 to 1975, the structure and function of the tribal government were not clearly defined, but in 1975-76 the tribe wrote a constitution as "The Cherokee Nation of Oklahoma", and received federal recognition. (70) In 1999, the CNO changed or added several provisions to its constitution, among them the designation of the tribe to be "Cherokee Nation". Dropping "of Oklahoma".

The modern Cherokee Nation, in recent times, has experienced an almost unprecedented expansion in economic growth, equality, and prosperity for its citizens. The Cherokee Nation, under the leadership of Principal Chief Chad Smith, has significant business, corporate, real estate, and agricultural interests, including numerous highly profitable casino operations. The CN controls Cherokee Nation Entertainment, Cherokee Nation Industries, and Cherokee Nation Businesses, CNI is, a very large defense contractor that creates thousands of jobs in eastern Oklahoma for Cherokee citizens.

## Eastern Band of Cherokee Indians

Some Cherokees were able to evade removal, and they became the Eastern Band of Cherokee Indians. William Holland Thomas, a white storeowner and state legislator from Jackson County, North Carolina, helped over 600 Cherokee from Qualla Town obtain North Carolina, citizenship, which exempted them from forced removal. Over 400 other Cherokee either hid from Federal troops in the remote Snowbird Mountains, under the leadership of Tsali, or belonged to the former

Valley Towns area around the Cheoah River who negotiated to stay in North Carolina with the state government.

The Eastern Band of Cherokee Indians is a federally recognized Native American tribe in the United States of America. The Eastern Cherokee are descendants primarily of those persons listed on the Baker Rolls of Cherokee Indians. The Qualla Boundary, the current homeland of the Eastern Band of Cherokee Indians, get most of its money from a combination of Federal/ State funds, tourism, and the Harrah's Cherokee Casino, instituted in the early 1990s. The Eastern Band of Cherokee Indians is not affiliated with the Cherokee Nation or the United Keetoowah Band of Cherokee Indians in Oklahoma, beyond cultural and historical ties. In 2009, the total population of the Eastern Band of Cherokee Indians has been reported over 13,000.

*Milton E. Campbell*

# History of the Eastern Band of Cherokee Indians

The Eastern Band members are primarily descended from Cherokee who did not participate in the march of the Trail of Tears to Oklahoma Territory, primarily owing to the foresight of Chief Yonaguska, and the help of his adopted Caucasian son, William Holland Thomas. The Eastern Band of Cherokee Indians still practice many of the original ceremonies, and many prominent Cherokee historians are affiliated with, or members of the Eastern Band.

Tsali opposed the removal, and remained in the Cherokee Homeland with a small group of Cherokee who formed a rebellious resistance against the United States to thwart the removal of the Cherokee on the Trial of Tears. Tsail was eventually captured, and executed by the United States in exchange for the lives of the small band he protected who remained in the Cherokee Homeland and became the modern Eastern Band.

The Eastern Cherokee Indian Reservation, officially known as the Qualla Boundary, is located in western North Carolina, just south of Great Smoky Mountains National Park. The main part of the reservation lies in eastern Swain County and northern Jackson County, but there are many small non-contiguous sections to the southwest in Cherokee County and Graham County. Also, a very small part of the main reservation extends eastward into Haywood County. The total land area of these parts is 82.600 square miles with a 2000 census resident population of 8, 092 persons.(71)

The Museum of the Cherokee Indian hosts and exhibits and extensive collection of artifacts and items of historical and cultural interest, from the early Mississippian Period through modern times, related to the Cherokee Culture. The Cherokee Heritage Center displays historical artifacts related to the march of the Cherokee on the Trial of Tears and the development of Oklahoma Cherokee Culture. When you visit Cherokee, North Carolina you can almost imagine yourself living this way. Here, the same mountains where the Cherokees have maintained their traditions for generations surround you. The Cherokees are people who proudly preserve a culture far older than the new nation that surrounds them.

# CHAPTER VI

## Lumbee Indians are descendants of the Cheraw and Siouan speaking tribes

The Lumbee are a Native American tribe that was recognized by the State of North Carolina as Croatan Indians in 1885. The Lumbee claim to be descendants of the Cheraw and related Siouan-speaking tribes of Native Americans originally inhabiting the coastal regions of the state of North Carolina. Some members of the lumbee tribe claim descent from the Cherokee or Tuscarora. The United States Congress passed House Resolution known as the Lumbee Act in 1956, which recognized the Lumbee as American Indians. The Lumbee Act specifically prohibited the Lumbee from receiving federal services ordinarily provided to federally recognized tribes through the Bureau of Indian Affairs.

## History of the Lumbee

The area of North Carolina today occupied by the Lumbee is called Robeson County. Robeson County was part of Bladen County until 1787. Governor Matthew Rowan dispatched surveying parties in 1753 to count Indians in the state, the final report stated that there were no Indians in the county.

According to colonial tax records from 1768 to 1770 the only Indian identified in Bladen County was Thomas Britt. Inhabitants of Bladen County characteristically Lumbee names were classified as "Mullato" in the tax records. Drawing from a wide variety of historical documents, in the late 20th century, genealogical researcher Paul Heinegg traced

Milton E. Campbell

the 35 mulatto families listed on the 1768-1770 Bladen County tax rolls and 24 other free families listed as Robeson County residents in the 1790-1800 censuses. He was able to trace them back to ancestors identified as free persons and referred to as Negro or Mulatto in Virginia or North Carolina. The free people of color were mostly descendants of white English women and African men who worked and lived together in colonial times. Their children were free because the legal status of the mother.

A colonial proclamation in 1773 listed the names of Robeson County inhabitants who took part in a "Mob Railously Assembled together," apparently defying the efforts of colonial officials to collect taxes. The proclamation declared that "the Above list of Rogus", which included many names since defined as characteristically Lumbee, "is all Free Negors and Mullatus living upon the Kings Land." A colonial military survey described, "50 families a mix crew a lawless People possess the Lands without Patent or paying quit Rents." (72)

In the first federal census of 1790, the ancestors of the Lumbee were among those enumerated as "free persons of color", a category used to describe free Negroes and mulattoes, and meaning freed African slaves or free descendants of mixed-race unions. In subsequent censuses, they were counted in "all other free person" or, later, "Mulatto." In the 1870 census, the first in which "Indian" was a separate category, almost all Robeson County residents with characteristically Lumbee names were classified as "Mulatto".

In 1835, North Carolina adopted a new constitution abolishing the right for free people of color to vote, which had been granted to them by the 1776 constitution. Judge Gaston of Craven stated that the majority of free persons of color in North Carolina during the colonial period were the descendants of white women who had unions with blacks and were entitled to all the rights of free men. The legislature rejected Craven's argument and took away the citizens right to vote of free people of color, regardless of their maternal ancestry, property holdings or literacy.(73)

*In 1840 thirty-six white Robeson County residents signed a petition that Robeson County had been cursed by the presence of what they described as being free colored population that migrated originally from the districts near the Roanoke and Neuse rivers. The first recorded reference to members of mixed race population as Indian dates from 1867, after the American Civil War.*

## 18th Century

*In 1754, a surveying party reported that Anson County was "a frontier to the Indians." Bladen County abutted Anson County which at that time extended west into Cherokee territory. The same report claimed no Indians lived in Bladen County which at that time contained what today is Robeson County. Land patents and deeds filed with the colonial administrations of Virginia, North and South Carolina during this period show that Lumbee ancestors were migrating into southern North Carolina along the typical routes of colonial migration from Virginia and obtaining land deeds in the same manner as any other migrants. In the first federal census of 1790, the ancestors of the Lumbee were enumerated as Free Persons of Color (74)*

The Lumbee ancestor James Lowrie received sizable land grant early in the 18th century and by 1738 possessed combined estates of more than two thousand acres. Dial and Eliades claimed that John Brooks established title to over one thousand acres in 1735, and Robert Lowrie gained possession of almost seven hundred acres. (75) However, a state archivist has noted that no land grants were issued during these years in North Carolina. The first land grants to documented Lumbee ancestors did not take place until more than a decade later, in the 1750's.(76)

The Lumbee petition for federal recognition use Land records show that beginning in the second half of the 18th century, ancestral Lumbees took titles to land described in relation to Drowning Creek and prominent swamps such as Ashpole, Long, and Back Swamp.(77) The Lumbee settlement with the longest continuous documentation from the mid-

*eighteenth century onward is Long Swamp, or present-day Prospect, North Carolina. Prospect is located within Pembroke and Smith townships. The Lumbee Indians are still in the process of seeking federal recognition and presently awaiting on the United State Senate to rule on this matter.*

*The State of North Carolina with Native American Ancestry*

Lake Waccamaw Siouan Dancers

# CHAPTER VII

## Haliwa-Soponi Indians from Halifax and Warren Counties

In eastern North Carolina you will find the home of the Haliwa-Saponi Indians, one of eight Native American tribes recognized by the state. The Haliwa-Saponi holds membership on the North Carolina Commission of Indian Affairs. Halifax and Warren counties are ancestral homelands of the Haliwai-Saponi Indians. They were granted state recognition in 1965. The tribe added Saponi to their name in 1979, therefore, reflecting their descent from the Saponi, Tuscarora, and Nansemond peoples of present-day Virginia and the Carolinas.

## Demographics of the Haliwa-Saponi

The Haliwa-Saponi has more that 4,000 members actively enrolled in there tribe. About seventy percent of their tribal members live in Halifax and Warren counties. Also, you will find tribal members residing in Nash and Franklin Counties. The Indian communities have known it for many years that the Haliwa-Saponi host one of the largest Pow-Wows in the state of North Carolina, held annually the third weekend in April.

The United States Census of 2000 state that their is approximately 2,738 Native Americans reside in Halifax and Warren counties, which represent 3.5% of the total combined population. Over the last 20 years, the Native American population of the two counties increased by 48 percent. During the same time, the Black population increased by 15 percent, and the Hispanic population increased 50 percent, and the White population decreased by 5%.

Milton E. Campbell

## History of the Haliwa Saponi

*The Haliwa-Saponi is a Siouan-descent Native American tribe of North America's Southeastern Piedmont. John Lederer, a German surveyor, in 1670 visited a Saponi settlement along the Staunton River in southern Virginia. Thirty years later, John Lawson, commissioned by the Lords Proprietor to survey the Carolina colony's interior, encountered groups of Saponi as they conducted trade. Throughout the post-contact period of increasing English colonial settlement and expansion, southeastern Siouan Piedmont peoples such as the Saponi maintained autonomous villages in what is now northeastern North Carolina and southern Virginia. During the late seventeenth century, the Saponi undertook a political alliance with the culturally related Tottero, or Tutelo, and together comprised the Nassaw Nation.*

## Eighteenth Century

*The Haliwa Saponi had a continuous warfare with the Haudenosaunee and repeated outbreaks of infectious disease reduce the once populous Saponi. Joining with the Tottero and the Occaneechi, the Saponi migrated to northeastern North Carolina to be closer to the center of Virginia's colonial trade. In 1711, the Carolina colony went to war with the powerful Tuscarora Confederacy. With the defeat of the Tuscarora two year later, the Saponi and their closest allies met in Williamsburg with the Tuscarora and Nottoway to discuss the terms of peace. They entered into a new treaty of trade with Virginia's governor, Alexander Spotswood. Despite the success in treaty-making and tribal coalescence, the years between 1709 and 1714 were extremely difficult, with continuing population decline due to disease.*

## Migrations

*In 1740 the Saponi moved to north to Pennsylvania and New York, where they joined with the Iroquois for protection. After the American Revolutionary War and victory by the colonists, they moved with the Iroquois to Canada, where the British government provided land and some relocation assistance to their allies. This was the last time in which the Saponi tribe appeared in the historical record. (78) Tribal leaders stated by 1802 that their entire tribal people had moved and that any remaining Saponi in the South were no longer considered part of the tribe, as they would have intermarried with other races.*

*During the 1730's to the 1770's, Haliwa-Saponi ancestors settled in and near the modern Haliwa-Saponi area in North Carolina. The community began coalescing in "The Meadows" of southwestern Halifax County, North Carolina immediately after the American Revolution.*

## Nineteenth Century

*During the early 1900s, ancestral Haliwa-Saponi remained relatively isolated in the Meadows. They attempted to live peaceably alongside their neighbors. The 1830s. when the United States enforced policies to remove all Indians east of the Mississippi River, the federal government basically ignored most of the relatively landless and powerless small tribes settled in the southeastern Coastal Plain. However, Haliwa-Saponi tribal elders tell of several families migrating west to Indian Territory on their own, some merging into the general population, while others were adopted by one of the so called Five Civilized Tribes in Oklahoma. Over the course of the 1800s, the Haliwa-Saponi maintained a close, tight-nit tribal community in modern Halifax, Warren, Nash, and Franklin counties.*

*Milton E. Campbell*

## **Twentieth Century**

*In the late 20th century, Paul Heinegg's extensive research in colonial records revealed the origins of many free people of color in Virginia, North Carolina and the Chesapeake Bay Colony. Some free African Americans were descended from slaves who were freed as early as the 17th century. But, most descended from unions of white women, indentured or free, and African or African American men, indentured, free or slave. There were also some indentured men from present-day India and Pakistan who intermarried with European and African Women. Some of the few Native Americans who adopted English customs also married into these families or to English settlers. (79)*

*In many cases these free families migrated to frontier areas of Virginia and North Carolina, along with European neighbors, to purchase land and be relatively removed from the racial strictures of the coastal plantation areas. In North Carolina, free people of color could vote until a few decades into the nineteenth century. In some areas, the lighter-skinned descendants communities known as tri-racial isolates, where they intermarried for generation. (79) Some of these groups, like the Haliwa-Saponi, have identified as Native American and succeeded in gaining recognition as tribes by North Carolina and Virginia.*

*Federal recognition through the Interior Department's Bureau of Indian Affairs Office of Federal Acknowledgement remains a top priority for the Haliwa-Saponi. Presently, they are seeking and compiling additional information to respond to the Office of Federal Acknowledgement . The Tribe continues to perform research, update files, and monitor the federal acknowledgement process.*

# Chapter VIII

## Occaneechi *Indian are related to the Saponi and Tutelo*

*The Native American tribe that is related to the Saponi or Sappony and the Tuelo or Totero is the Occaneechi or Occoneechee Indians. These eastern Siouan language people live in the Piedmont region of present day North Carolina and Virginia. Siouan language peoples included those elements who migrated west to the Plains hundreds of years before European contact. The Eastern Siouan territory or nation also encompassed the majority of the current day states of Virginia and North Carolina along with half the state of South Carolina and parts of Georgia, West Virginia, and Ohio.*

*The Occoneechi lived on a large four mile long Island surrounded by the Dan and Roanoke rivers near current day Clarksville, Virginia. In 1676 the tribe was attacked by European settlers and decimated. Also under demographic pressure from European settlement and newly introduced infectious diseases, the Saponi and Tutelo came to live near them on adjacent islands. By 1714 the Occoneechee were grouped with the Totero, and Saponi, and other Siouan people living on a 36 square mile reservation in current day Brunswick County, Virginia. It included a fort called Christanna and the Siouan people had been drastically reduced to approximately 600 people. In 1717 Fort Christanna was closed, after which there are few written references to the Occaneechi. They were recorded as leaving the area in 1740 and migrating north for protection with the Iroquois.*

*The Occaneechi Band of the Saponi Nation today consists of about 900 tribal members living primarily in Alamance County, North Carolina. In 2002 it was the most recent tribe to be recognized by the state of North Carolina.*

*Milton E. Campbell*

## History of the Occaneechi Indians

The colonial English records mention the Occaneechi Indians as living on the Trading Path that connected Virginia to the interior of North America. In 1673, Abraham Wood, a Virginian fur trader, sent James Needham and Gabriel Arthur into the southern Appalachian Mountains in an attempt to make direct contact with the Cherokee, thus by passing the Occaneechi. It was not until colonial South Carolina established a strong relationship with the Cherokee and other interior tribes in the last decades of the $17^{th}$ century that the Occaneechi's role as trading middleman was undermined. (80) In 1701 John Lawson visited Occaneechi Town on the Eno River. His written report plus modern archaeology at the site paint a picture of a society undergoing rapid change while trying to maintain their traditional way of life. The Occaneechi, along with the "Stuckanok, Tottero, and Saponi," signed a "Treaty of Peace" with the colony of Virginia in 1713. They then moved to Fort Christanna in southeast Virginia. The Occaneechi Town appeared to have been almost entirely abandoned by 1713. The Virginia Company from 1714 to 1717 operated Fort Christanna. Its closure was due to a lack of profits via its use as an Indian trading center. Although several distinct groups of Siouan Indians lived at Fort Christanna, the English Virginians tended to refer to them simply as "Saponi" or "Fort Christanna Indians." Virginia's House of Burgesses records in 1730 note an "Interpreter to the Saponi and Occaneechi Indians," implying the existence of monoglot Occaneechi people. In 1730, many Saponi moved to live among the Catawba, but returned to Virginia in 1733, along with some Cheraw Indians. After 1733 the Saponi appear to have fragmented into small groups and dispersed. Some apparently remained in the vicinity of Fort Christanna, which continued to be mentioned in Virginian records by its Saponi name Junkatapurse. After 1742 the settlement is no longer mentioned, but only a road called Junkatapurse. In the 1740s, the Saponi again went to live with the Catawba, Governor Gooch of Virginia reported that thee "Saponies and other petty nations associated with them are retired out of Virginia to the Cattawbas" during the years 1743-1747.(80) The remaining Saponi tribe members were recorded as migrating north in 1740 for protection with the Iroquois. They disappeared from the historical record in the Southeast. After the American Revolution, in which they sided with the British, the majority of the Iroquois and Saponi went to Canada for resettlement.

During the middle of the 18$^{th}$ century, there are records of Saponi living in North Carolina. They had moved from Virginia to various places in North Carolina. There is some evidence that isolated Indians never left these areas of North Carolina and became consolidated with Saponi from Virginia. In 1763, Lt. Governor Francis Fauqier of Virginia wrote a letter including a description of the Indians of Virginia. "There are some of the Nottoways, Meherrins, Tuscaroras, and Saponys, who live in peace in the midst of us, lead in great measure the lives of wild Indians."(80) He contrasted these Indians with the Eastern Shore and Pamunkey Indians, whom he described as more assimilated to English ways. Traditional English-American histories typically describe the Saponi group of Indians as having left Virginia and North Carolina in the 1700s, either to join the Catawbas or the Iroquois.

# Chapter IX

*Meherrin Indian Tribe is of the same linguistic stock as the Cherokee and Tuscarora*

The Meherrin Indian Tribe is of the same linguistic stock as the Cherokee, Tuscarora, and other tribes of the Iroquois Confederacy of New York and Canada. These Native American people of North America spoke a language that was very similar to the Tuscarora dialect. The tribal name "Meherin" means "People of the Muddy Water" or the "Muddy Water People". The Europeans used various spellings of the Meherrin Tribal name in documents and historical writings. These spellings include Maherineck, Maherrins, Menheyricks, Maherine, Meherin, Meahearin, Meheren, Macherine, Maherring, Meherron, Maherin and Meharins. An English merchant named Edward Bland, along with five other Englishmen, one Nottoway Indian and one Appomattox Indian arrived on August 29th 1650 in the Meherrin village of Cowonchahawkon on the north bank of the Meherrin River, two miles west of the present day city of Emporia, Virginia. They also found to more villages in the same vicinity and they were called Taurura which is near present day Boykins, Virginia and the village of Unote, which was on the Meherrin River between Emporia and Boykins. The Emporia area provided basically all the materials that the Meherrin needed to survive. The land, rive, streams and creeks provided fish for this native tribe in order to sustain life along with the wild game. The written history of the Meherrin Indian Tribe began in Virginia, however, it did not take long before the pressures of the colonists and traditional Indian enemies forced the Meherrin Indians further down the Meherrin River into Hertford County, North Carolina. The tribe settled at the mouth of the Meherrin

*Milton E. Campbell*

*River around 1706, on a reservation site that had been abandoned by the Chowannoke Indian Tribe.*

*The steady encroachment of colonists onto the reservation and European introduced diseases, the Meherrin Indians left the reservation and migrated into the surrounding swamps and less desirable areas of Hertford County. After becoming individual landowners, the Meherrin Indians had to conceal their identity in order to survive in the racial climate of the era. Racial prejudice prevented the Meherrin Indians from reorganizing in the late 1800's and early 1900's, however, the events of the time prejudices, friction in the community, governmental interference prevented the Tribe from openly acknowledging its continued existence and Indian heritage. In 1977, the Meherrin Indian Tribe charted itself as a nonprofit organization under the leadership of the late Chief Rueben R. Lewis. During the 1970s, the Meherrin Indians directed most of their energies toward cultural awareness, state recognition, and eventual Federal Recognition as a tribe. The North Carolina Commission of Indian Affairs granted state recognition to the Meherrin Indian Tribe in 1986.*

*Presently, the Meherrin Indian Tribe is located in Hertford County, North Carolina about 10 miles from their original reservation. The Tribe maintains it's tribal traditions and heritage by celebrating with an annual Pow Wow. The Tribe meets throughout the year and on other occasions such as Thanksgiving and Christmas or just to have a family day. The Tribe holds monthly general body and council meetings in order to maintain tribal governance within the tribal entity.(81)*

# Chapter X

## *Tuscarora Indian Tribe*

*The Tuscarora are a Native American Indian Tribe with members in Canada, North Carolina and New York. This Native American Tribe emigrated from the region now known as Western New York to the region now know as Eastern Carolina prior to the arrival of Europeans in North America and Virginia. (82) After many wars during the 18th century, most of the Tuscarora left North Carolina and aligned with the Iroquois in New York. However, a significant minority remained in North Carolina without a formal government or reservation land.*

## *History of the Tuscarora Indians*

*During the 17th and early 18th century there were two primary contingents of the Tuscarora tribe located in North Carolina. The northern group led by Chief Tom Blunt, and a southern group led by Chief Hancock (82). The area around what is present day Bertie County, North Carolina, on the Roanoke River is where Chief Blunt occupied. The area closer to New Bern and south of the Pamlico River is the territory that Chief Blunt controlled. Chief Hancock found his villages raided and his people frequently kidnapped and sold into slavery. Both groups were heavily impacted by the introduction of European diseases, and both were rapidly having their lands stolen by the encroaching colonists. Finally, Chief Hancock felt there was no alternative but to attack the settlers. The southern Tuscarora, led by Chief Hancock worked in conjunction with the Pamlico, the Coree, Cothechney, the Mattamuskeet and the Matchepungoe nations to attack* the settlers in a wide range of locations in a short time period. The main targets were the on the Roanoke River, the planters on the Neuse and Trent Rivers and the city of Bath. On September 22, 1711, this was the first attack and hundreds of settlers were ultimately killed. After several attacks Governor Edward Hyde called out the militia of North Carolina and secured the assistance of the Legislature of South Carolina, who provided six hundred militia and three hundred sixty allied Native Americans under Col. Barnwell. This force attacked the southern Tuscarora and other nations in Craven County at Fort Narhantes on the banks of the Neuse River in 1712, The Tuscarora were defeated with great slaughter and more than three hundred were killed and one hundred made prisoners. After this slaughter, Chief Blunt was offered the chance to control the entire Tuscarora Nation if assisted the settlers in putting down Chief Hancock. Chief Blunt was able to capture Chief Hancock, and the settlers executed him in 1712. In 1713 the Southern Tuscarora's lost Fort Neoheroka, with 900 soles killed or captured. After this lost, the majority of the Southern Tuscarora began migrating to New York to escape the settlers in North Carolina. The migration took place approximately over a 90 year span, however, significant numbers of Tuscarora continued to live in North Carolina, some openly, and others in hiding. At the end of the Tuscarora War (1711-1715), most of the nation moved from North Carolina to New York where they joined the Five Nations Iroquois Confederacy. They settled near the sponsoring Oneidas. Originally the Tuscarora Indians were part of a group of ancient Iroquoian nations originating in the Lake Ontario and Lake Eric regions, so they were reuniting with tribes familiar to them. The remaining Tuscarora signed a treaty with the North Carolina settlers in June 1718 granting them a tract of land on the Roanoke River in what is now Bertie County. This was the area already occupied by Tom Blunt and was specified as 56,000 acres. The remaining Southern Tuscarora were removed from their homes on the Pamlico River and made to move to Bertie. In 1722, the Bertie County reservation was chartered. Over the next several decades, the remaining Tuscarora lands were continually diminished as they were sold off in deals that were frequently designed to take advantage of the Tuscarora.(82)

*In New York, part of the Tuscarora and Oneida nation sided against the rest of the Iroquois Confederacy by fighting for the newly established Colonial government during the American Revolutionary War. Most of those Indians who remained allies of Great Britain later followed Joseph Brant into Ontario. In 1803 the final contingent of the Tuscarora migrated to New York to re-join with the nation at their reservation in Niagara County, under a treaty directed by Thomas Jefferson. However, Jefferson never ratified the 1803 treaty, so the North Carolina Tuscarora view the treaty as null and void. In 1832 the Tuscarora in North sold the remaining rights to their lands. This point had pared down the 56,000 acres to a mere 2,000 acres. However, despite not having a reservation territory in North Carolina significant numbers of Tuscarora remain there, a fact which the federal government acknowledges.(83)*

## 20$^{th}$ Century

*In the 20th century, city commissioner Robert Moses expropriated 550 acres of Tuscarora reservation land for a hydroelectric project in the vicinity of Niagara Falls, New York. Various bands of the Tuscarora have worked for federal and state recognition. Efforts include the petition by the Hatteras Tuscarora in the 1970s, which was unsuccessful. In 2006 the Skaroreh Katenuaka Nation or the Tuscarora "Nation of Indians of North Carolina" filed a federal lawsuit for recognition. It is the dream of the Tuscarora Indians that in the future, they will obtain state recognition in North Carolina and then Federal Recognition from the United State Government.(84)*

# Chapter XI

## *Waccamaw Siouan Indians are located in Bladen and Columbus counties*

Waccamaw Siouan Indian is a tribal nation located predominantly in the southeastern North Carolina counties of Bladen and Columbus. The communities with a strong influence of Waccamaw Siouan tribal members are St. James, Buckhead, and Council. The tribal homeland of the Waccamaw Siouan is situated on the edge of Green Swamp and about 38 miles from Wilmington, North Carolina. The Waccamaw Siouan Indians are one of eight state recognized Native American tribal nations in North Carolina.(85)

## *Demographics*

The 2000 Census of the United States of America stated that the total Waccamaw Siouan Native American population in Columbus and Bladen Counties was 2,343. This represents 2.7 % of the total combined Native American population of North Carolina. The Current tribal enrollment consists of 1,245 tribal members. Between 1980 and 2000 Bladen and Columbus counties experienced a small overall population increase of 6.7% compared with a 37% rate of growth for North Carolina. The predominant growth that took place in the Native American and Hispanic populations. Also, both counties saw a 7% increase in the Afro-American population and a .6% decrease in the white population.(87)

Milton E. Campbell

## History of the Lake Waccamaw Siouan Indians

In 1521 the Spanish expedition led by Francisco Girebillo came across a Waccamwaw village which he describe as semi-nomadic river basin inhabitants. Girebillo expedition arrived there by traveling inland form the Carolina coast and along the Waccamaw and Pee Dee River. Girebillo wrote that Siouan river peoples relied on hunting and gathering, and to some extent, a limited agriculture. (88) Nearly 150 years later, William Hilton encountered the Waccamaw Siouan and in 1670, the German surveyor and physician, John Lederer, mentioned them in his Discoveries. By the beginning of the seventeenth century the Woccon or Waccamaw along with a number of Pee Dee River tribes, had been pushed north by a combination of Spanish and Cusabo forces. Settling around the confluence of the Waccamaw and Pee Dee River, this amalgam of tribes had already fragmented by 1705 to form a group of Woccon who moved farther north to the Lower Neuse River and Contentnea Creek.(89)

## Eighteenth Century

The English Colonials recorded first mention the Waccamaw or Woccon Indians in 1712. During this period the South Carolina Colony attempted to persuade the Waccamaw, along with the Cape Fear Indians, to join the son of the former British colonial governor of South Carolina , Mr. James Moore, in his expedition against the Tuscarora in the Tuscarora War. In 1670 John Lederer and some thirty years later John Lawson referred to the Waccamaw in their travel narratives as an Eastern Siouan peoples. The Siouan remain, neither man visited the wetlands to which some of the Waccamaw were beginning to seek refuge from colonial incursions. The Siouan tribe or Woccon Indians that John Lawson had placed a few miles to the south of the Tuscarora in his" New Voyage to Carolina", written in 1700. As the Woccon Indians continue to move southward they were later identified as Waccamaw in colonial records. Since differing colonial powers could only approximate the sound of the names of numerous southeastern indigenous polities, tribal names were often arbitrarily changed or altered in their spelling. In historical records at the same time Woccon disappeared Waccamaw appeared.

The region along the Waccamaw and Pee Dee River was continued to be inhabit by the Waccamaw Indians until 1718. In 1720, the tribe joined with fleeing families of Tuscarora, Cheraw, Keyauwee, and Hatteras Indians along Drowing creek, now known as the Lumber River. Until 1733, families of Waccamaw Indians continued to live in the area of Drowning Creek, and some families moved and sought refuge along Lake Waccamaw and Green Swamp located in present day Columbus and Bladen counties.

By 1749 many Waccamaw, also known as the Waccommassus, were located one hundred miles northeast of Charleston, South Carolina. After the 1749, war between the Waccamaw and South Carolina Colony it was twenty nine year later in May 1778, provisions were made by the Council of South Carolina to render the Waccamaw protection, however, the colony didn't keep there promise. Therefore, the Waccamaw sought refuge in the wetland region situated on the edge of Green Swamp, near Lake Waccamaw. The tribe eventually settled four miles north of Bolton, North Carolina along what is still known as the "Old Indian Trial.(90)

## 19$^{th}$ century

The oral tradition of the Waccamaw Siouan Indians and their claim to the Green Swamp region has been proven to be correct thru North Carolina state land deeds and colonial records. Three century long historical experience of European contact, the Waccamaw Siouan Indians had become highly acculturated. They tribe depended on European style agriculture and established claims to land through individuated farmsteads.(91)

In 1835, the Waccamaw Siouan Indians were disenfranchised when the state passed amendments to its original constitution of 1776. The Waccamaw Siouan Indians were classified as free people of color and were stripped of their political and civil rights, therefore, could not vote, bear arms, or serve in the state militia.(92)

## 20$^{th}$ century

During the 20$^{th}$ century the Waccamaw Siouan Indians have maintain a long tradition of affiliation with other tribal nations. The Waccamaw Siouan also continues to intermarriage with other tribes. Surnames found among the Waccamaw Siouan are Jacob, Young, Webb, Campbell, Freeman, Patrick, Graham, Hammond, Blanks, Hunt, Locklear, Moore, Mitchell and Strickland. For example, Hugh Campbell born October 28,1919 in Bladen County, North Carolina, son of Roland Campbell born in 1892 and Mattie Spaulding Campbell born, March 8, 1890 was a member of the Siouan Nation. Children of Hugh Campbell who married Bertie Mitchell Campbell are tribal members of the Waccamaw Siouan and they live in the St. James Community. Benjamin Spaulding(1878-1962) son David Spaulding has been identified in North Carolina death records has a Native American and he lived in the St. James Community until his death. Benjamin Spaulding(1878-1962) was instrumental in establishing the Hickory Hill Indian School in 1925. Benjamin Spaulding understood that Native American People had to get their education that had been denied for so many years. There are many Waccamaw Siouan Indian living in the Farmer Union Community who was denied tribal membership due to the fact they don't live in the Waccamaw Siouan Indian Territory or they don't participate in tribal affairs. The Farmer Union Siouan Indians are presently seeking separate state recognition from the Lake Waccamaw Siouan in Bolton, North Carolina. The Lake Waccamaw Siouan Indians received state recognition in 1971 and are presently work on Federal recognition.(93)

*It is possible that some of the Lake Waccamaw Siouan tribe banded together with other remnant Native America Tribes that were fleeing for their safety during the 18th century. This was a difficult time in history when many native people were forced to move from their homeland for survival. Native tribes banded together and tried to protect their people especially the Indian tribes in North Carolina.*

*We are in the 21th century and it is time for all Native American people to come together and work together as we move into the future, following the tradition of our ancestors.*

Lake Waccamaw Siouan Pow Wow

Lila Mitchell Spaulding (1931-  )

# Chapter XII

*Surnames: Campbell, Graham, Jacobs, Spaulding, Blanks, and Moore.*

## Origin of the Surname Campbell

*Sir Cailein Mor Campbell's grandfather Dugaldon Lochawe who is said to have been the first given the nickname "Cam Buel" since had the engaging trait of talking out of one side of his mouth. Cam Buel means curved mouth in the Gaelic. Originally the spelling of the surname was Cambel. Then when Robert and Bruce's son King David came to the throne as King of Scots he brought with him a number of Norman knights to whom he gave lands in an attempt to introduce Norman efficiency in administration. David had been at the English court and admired the Norman system of feudalism. The use of the spelling "Campbell" may perhaps have been as a result of Norman rather than Gaelic scribes attempting to write the Gaelic name. The name Cambel was first used by the family in the $13^{th}$ century. The first chief of the clan to appear on record as "Campbell" may well have been Sir Ducan of Lochawe when he was created Lord Campbell in 1445.*

## Campbell Ancestors

*Campbell castles and lands could be found in six parts of Scotland: Argyll, Angus, Ayrshire, Clackmannan, Nairnshire and Perthshire, although principally in Argyll where the home of the Chief, Inveraray Castle, is the most important to any Campbell visitor. The castle at Inveraray is open to the public in the summer season, except on Fridays.*

Argyll is a county of about 100 miles in length north to south and slightly less in width. The coastline is over 1,000 miles in length including the inhabited islands. Tradition holds that the first of the Campbell ancestors who came into Argyll married Eva, daughter of Paul and Sporran and the heiress of the O'Duibne tribe on northwestern Lochawe. This ancestor may well have been established in Argyll as a follower of the Earl of the neighboring Lennox when Alexander II, king of Scots, marched into Argyll to ensure the loyalty of its people. Alexander is said by Fordun, a Medieval writer, to have visited Argyll in 1222, and this period for a Campbell ancestral arrival on Lochawe is supported by the Gaelic genealogies and later charters. The first of the name Cambel which was the original spelling can be found in the surviving records was one who owned lands near Sterling in 1263. The earliest written date for a Camel in Argyll is that for Duncan Dubh, landowner in Kintyre in 1293. The first date which survives for the Cambels on Lochawe is that for the Killing of Sir Cailein Mor(Great Colin) of Lochawe in 1296 when he was attacked by men of the Clan Dougall on the Stringe of Lorne. His family had been long established on Lochawe and at that time at least two other Cambels owned land in Argyll and they were Sir Duncan Dubh and Sir Thomas in Kintyre.( 94)

## Samuel Campbell Family from Bladen County, North Carolina

The Campbell family has played many roles in the development of the two great nations of North America and Canada. Much of their influence remains to be documented but there is evident of strong influence in health, education, the military, exploration, industry, agriculture and governments.

Samuel Campbell was born around 1785 in Bladen County, North Carolina. He later married Euphemia Jacobs Campbell born in 1795. (95) To the union their were two children, Hugh Campbell and Caroline Campbell. It is thought that from Archival Research in Bladen County, North Carolina that Samuel Campbell grandfather and their families were of Highland Scots decent that migrated to Bladen County, North Carolina. In 1739, Gabriel Johnston, royal governor of North

Carolina and native Scotsman, encouraged 360 Highlands Scots to settle in North Carolina and later provided them a ten-year tax exemption for doing so. Subsequent offers by Johnston attracted Highland Scots to North Carolina primarily for economic and political reasons, for in Scotland, they had difficulties paying the increasing land rents and experienced defeat against the English at the Battle of Culloden in 1745. Many Highland Scots migrated to North America begin in 1700s until the 1800s. They settle mainly in North Carolina but many sailed to New York, New Jersey Georgia, and Canada. North Carolina records reveal that countless Highland Scots migrated to North Carolina during the colonial period. Arriving in Wilmington, most who came had obtained a land grant from the government to settle in the Upper Cape region, because they knew many parts of the Lower Caper Fear had been settled. In 1754, enterprising merchants from Wilmington had settled Cross Creek, and interior town on the Cape Fear River, so many Highlanders dwelled near the small creeks flowing into the river. Highland settlements were numerous in this region during the eighteenth century, and evidence of them can be seen today in Anson, Bladen, Moore, Cumberland, Richland, Scotland, and Robeson counties.

The Lowland Scots who migrated from Scotland to North Carolina in the eighteenth century primarily settled in the Lower Cape Fear region around Wilmington, North Carolina. The 1790 census lists 150 inhabitants of the Upper Cape Fear Valley who named Scotland as their birthplace. Unlike Highlanders in other colonies, those in North Carolina intermarried with Lowland Scots. Also, there is strong evident that Samuel Campbell born in 1785 grandfather was a white man from Scotland, who had a relationship with a Native American Women, who was mostly likely was from the Siouan Tribe. Samuel Campbell grandfather most likely was a Lowland Scot who had arrived to North America in the mid -1700s. In the 1850 census, Samuel Campbell lived in the Cape Fear South Township located in Bladen County, North Carolina. Also in 1850, Samuel Campbell son Hugh Campbell (1827-1860) was living in Cape Fear South Township, and he had married Dorcus Freeman and they were proud parents of three children. They were Stephen Campbell, Amy Campbell, Martha Campbell.

*Milton E. Campbell*

*Samuel grandson Stephen Campbell was born in 1846, the son of Hugh Campbell lived also in the Cape Fear South Township according to the 1850 census of Bladen County. They are all listed as mulattos and were free people of color according to the 1850 Census of the United States, which means they were of mix ancestry. (95) This area at the time the Highlanders arrived was occupied by many remnants of Native American Tribes.*

*According to James Sprunt in Chronicles of the Cape Fear River 1660-1916 he refer to the Woccon, Saxapahaw, Cape Fear, and Warrennuncock Indians. The Cape Fear Indians was name by the early colonists who found them occupying the lands about the mouth of the Cape Fear River, and more especially the peninsula now forming the southern part of New Hanover County. It is also possible the term Cape Fear Indians was applied to any Indians found in the vicinity, regardless of their tribal connections. The Bladen County area was frequented by numbers of different tribes. It is very likely that Samuel Campbell mother could have belong to one of these early Native American tribes that are listed in James Sprunt Chronicles.*

*Euphemia Jacobs (1795-1866) the wife of Samuel Campbell is also though to be of Native American Ancestry according to family members. The ancestors of Samuel Campbell (1785 -1853) were mixed with white and Indian blood. Samuel grandson in 1870, Stephan Campbell moved to whites Creek Township where he married Edith Spaulding Campbell, daughter of Henry Spaulding son of Benjamin Spaulding (1773-1862) from Duplin County, North Carolina. (96)*

*In 1732 in the General Assembly there were attempts to make two new precincts, Onslow and Bladen from the larger precinct of New Hanover. It was stated by the council that in Bladen Precinct that there are not over three freeholders, Nathaniel Moore, Thomas Jones, and Richard Singletary, and not over 30 families, including these freeholders. The Campbell family was one of the 30 families that lived in Bladen Precinct according to North Carolina Land Grants and state deeds. Bladen Precinct was recognized on November 11, 1734* but not without resistance brought by the Council in Edenton, North Carolina. In 1739 all precincts in North Carolina were re-labeled as counties.

According to the 1790 census of Bladen County there were seven Campbell Families and the spelling of their last name were Camble; they are Archabald Camble, Daniel Camble, Alexander Camble, James Camble, John Camble, Neal Camble. They are all white men according to the 1790 census. Although earlier records were destroyed or not recorded, it is most likely that Samuel Campbell born in 1785 is a descendant of one of these families because they lived in close proximity to each other in Bladen County.

Samuel Campbell just like the early Scots was taught by his family to raised livestock, including sheep and swine, and grew wheat and corn while other Campbell relatives worked in industry. Samuel Campbell and his children were always identified as free mulatto's according to the earlier census of the United States of America.

Argylll Colony in the Cape Fear Valley of North Carolina was established in 1739. This moment in time was an important event which documents the history of Scotland and America. Archibald Campbell, an agent for the Argyll estate, observed that tenants in Kintyre were inspired by their Irish neighbors to leave for America. The island of Islay called by its native inhabitants came into the possession of Daniel Campbell, a Glasgow merchant and Member of Parliament. He decides to stay in Scotland rather to risk his fate in America. However, there is a person by the name of Daniel Campbell who could have been descendants of Campbell's from the island of Islay that arrived in Wilmington, North Carolina in 1774. However, there were other groups of Highlanders that came to America and established the Argyll Colony in 1740 around modern day Fayetteville, North Carolina.

In 1767 there was a large migration of Highlanders that flooded the Cape Fear valley of North Carolina. This group was from a larger area of Argyll, including the islands of Arran, Jura, Islay and Gigha. The development of worsening economic conditions in the 1770s, this force many of the Highlanders to migrate from Scotland to America.(97)

## Milton E. Campbell

The Campbell family name is associated with the Highlanders for many generations according to land deeds. It must be stated that the Campbell ancestors in America is of mixed blood. In the early years the Campbell families from Scotland integrated into the Native America populations of North America. This can be seen with in Samuel Campbell Family from Bladen County, North Carolina. He was born in 1785 and identified as a person of mix blood (Mulatto) in the 1850 census. Also, his son Hugh Campbell and his grandson Stephen Campbell, and his great grandson Roland Campbell born in 1892 were identified as Mulattos according to census records. The Scottish name Campbell can also be found predominantly among Whites in Robeson County. However, a few Blacks and a few Lumbee families carry this surname. The name was listed as Indian in Shoe Heel (Maxton) township in the 1870 Census of Robeson. It was self-identified as Indian in the 1900 Census Schedule. Death records show that the Indian name Campbell in 1925 and 1955, in Rowland, related to the Locklear family. A widow of Solomon Campbell, Mary Lillie Strong Campbell, who died in 2004, left Lumbee relatives named Hammonds, Hunt, Locklear and Bell. The Indian name Campbell also appears in Scotland County(2005). Cited by Jane Blanks Barnhill, SACRED GROUNDS, 2007, a listing of 162 Lumbee cemeteries in Robeson County.

Today, the Campbell families from Bladen and Roberson Counties, North Carolina have become a very successful across North America. Regardless of their racial background they have become very successful farmer, schoolteachers, lawyer, business leaders thru out the United States of America. Although, Daniel Campbell was a farmer from Scotland who is listed on the passenger list of the Ship Ulysses, which sailed from Greenock to Wilmington, North Carolina on August 1774, and Samuel Campbell Family of mix blood who was located in Cape Fear South region of Bladen County many year before Daniel Campbell arrived in Wilmington, North Carolina. There is strong evident thru land grants that the Campbell's were one of the first family to leave Scotland and come to America and to encounter the native people living in the Caper Fear region of North Carolina. (98)

## (1785 & 1795)
## Samuel Campbell & Euphemia Jacobs Campbell Descendants

Stephen Campbell
(1846-1910)

Roland Campbell Sr
(1892-1942)

Roland Campbell Jr.
(1917-2002)

Israel Samuel Campbell
(1879-1944)

Milton E. Campbell

## Origin of the Surname Graham

The surname Graham is found among the Lumbers and the Melungeons of Tennessee. In Robeson County it can be Lumbee but it is most often White. Before 1800, Robeson had deed records for Alexander, Archibald, Dugald, Ducan, John and Nancy Graham. Most often the name is Scottish in orgin. Alexander Graham was listed with 210 acres and 1 White Poll in the 1801 Tax list of Captain Watson's District. Graham was given as an Indian name in Alfordsville township in the 1870 census of Robeson. The name was self-identified as Indian in the 1900 Census of Robeson and listed in the 1900 Indian Census Schedule. The 1900 Directory of Robeson lists the name in Pembroke. Graham was also listed as Indian in the 1930 census of Pembroke Township. Death records show the Indian name of Graham in 1919 in Back Swamp, Lumberton and Pembroke townships. Noted at Deep Branch cemetery by Jane Blanks Barnhill, SACRED GROUNDS, 2007 a listing of 162 Lumbee cemeteries in Robeson County.

## The Graham Family from Bladen and Columbus Counties

William Graham was born about 1800 and first appeared in the census report of 1800 as being married to Sarah Graham born in 1802. William Graham and his wife Sarah live on the banks of the Cape Fear River on the south side. The locating where he lived can be identified as Indian Wells Landing in Bladen County, North Carolina . The family of Samuel Campbell and Elijah Blanks can also be found in the 1850 census of the United States of America living in this area. Graham, Blanks, and Campbell families are thought to be from predominantly the Siouan Stock of Native American Indians. William Graham and his wife along with his three children John, Henry, Jack is said to have been save from the extermination of the Native American Indian after order was give by the President of the United States Zachary Taylor to kill all Indians between the Carolinas and Florida. The colonists classified all Indians occupying the lands about the mouth of the Cape Fear River, and especially the peninsula now forming the southern part of New Hanover County as Cape Fear Indians regardless of their tribal affiliation. It has been well documented that that the Siouan people settled in the Green Swamp, Waccamaw River Banks, South Carolina and Lake Waccamaw. Reports were made by the United States Government that all Indians were exterminated during this time period, however, these reports are not correct because today we still see evidence of the Grahams, Campbell's, and Mitchells, Jacobs and Blanks families occupying this territory. It is mostly due to the dense forest and the ability of these native American families to adapt to the constant changing environment made it possible for them to sustain life. It must be stated, that the Grahams, Campbell's, Blanks and other families are listed as free inhabitants that lived in Bladen County, North Carolina according to earlier Bladen County Census Reports.

William Graham and his wife Sarah and their son John seem to have disappeared and there are not records on their survival. However, there are written records on Jack Graham and Henry Graham. Jack Graham married Eliza and there were nine children born to this union. Later, Jack Graham had to relinquish his homestead in exchange for his family's safety. After being force to leave his land Jack and his family migrated from the south side of the Cape Fear River (Indian Wells) in a canoe. During the journey Jack disappeared and may have been killed by his enemies. Eliza Graham and her children relocated to Steep Run in Columbus County, North Carolina where they lived in a small one-room hut. Many years later, some of the children of William and Sarah Graham move to the St. James community and intermarried with local families such as the Mitchell, Blanks, Mears, Freemans and Spaulding's. Bladen County records indicated that Henry Graham and Lucy Blanks Graham son Clifford Graham was born March 20, 1874 in Bladen County, North Carolina between East Arcadia and Carvers Creek in the small community now known as Youngtown. Clifford Graham parents are found buried in the family graveyard across the creek from what was called the Granny Winnie house. Clifford Graham died on July 25, 1947 and was buried at Graham's Methodist Church in the East Arcadia community. (99)

*Milton E. Campbell*

*William and Sarah Graham story is one of the greatest Native American Indian story of survival in Bladen County, North Carolina. Despite the odds against them this family survived and their descendants are still living predominantly in the St. James Community. The descendants of William and Sarah Graham are members of the Waccamaw Siouan Tribe which is located in Lake Waccamaw, Bolton, and Chadbourn, North Carolina. The Graham Family is part of a North Carolina State recognized tribe with over 2000 tribal members. The Graham Family also supports the Lake Waccamaw Siouan tribe in their effort to achieve Federal Recognition.*

## (1800 & 1802)
## William and Sarah Graham Descendants

Benjamin Graham (1860-1943)

James graham (1863-1946)

Sarah Graham

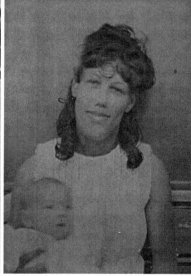
Mary S. Graham (1943-1968)

Milton E. Campbell

## Jacobs and Spaulding Surnames

The name Jacobs is frequently and stereotypically Lumbee in Robeson County. White(1988) feels that the Jacobs family descended from Saponi Indians who lived next to the plantation of Col. William Eaton in Granville County in the 1750s. The Lumbee name appears in the 1790 census of Sampson County and on tax lists of various North Carolina counties in 1752. William Jacobs was in Duplin up through 1785 when it became Sampson County. The Jacobs name does not appear in the 1775-1789 tax lists of Bladen County. James, Samuel and Shaderick Jacobs signed a petition regarding roadwork in current Bladen County on Waccamaw Lake on September 1, 1802. Although no Jacobs were listed as Bladen taxables in the 18$^{th}$ century, the 1850 census of Robeson had family members reporting that they had been born in Robeson County as early as 1775 and several in the early 1800s. Perhaps they simply failed to get listed or owned no land. Deed indexes for Robeson 1787-1939 show James Jacobs in 1826-1835, Mary Jacobs in 1829, Zachariah Jacobs in 1842, and William Jacobs in 1854. The name was self-identified as Indian in the 1900 Census of Robeson County. Listed in the 1900 Indian Census Schedule of Robeson County. Jacobs was listed as Indian in the 1930 census of Pembroke Township. The Lumbee name Jacobs was enrolled at Pembroke State University in 1924. Death records of 1916 and later show the Indian family of Jacobs in Back Swamp, Burnt Swamp, Gaddy, Pembroke, Smiths and Thompson's townships.

The surname Spaulding originated in the place called Spalding, in Lincolnshire. Spaulding is a Scottish surname, which belongs to the category of hereditary surnames. The earliest members of the Spaulding family on record, were found in Lincolnshire, where they settled on lands granted by William the Conqueror, following the Norman Invasion, in 1066. The Spaulding family rose to prominence in Scotland. There are many variations of this family name include Spaulding, Spalding, Spaldens and others that occur in early land deeds in Scotland and then later in America. Some of the first settlers of this family name to arrive in America were Edward Spalding who settled with his wife and two children in Virginia in 1623. Later, records indicate that Alex

Spalding settle in Maryland in 1716. It must be stated that today many times people in their search for their ancestors have discarded people who have a different spelling of their surname, only to find later that this was another example of history's very relaxed attitude to spelling. like the Spaulding name , often changes were made to make it easier for people to spell upon their arrival in the Americas.

The surname Spaulding was self-identified as Indian in the 1900 Census of Robeson County and was listed in the 1900 Indian Census Schedule for Robeson County. Death records show the name Spaulding from 1923 in Alfordsville, Fairmont and Rowland townships. They married into the Burleson, Chavis, Oxdendine, Rogers and Webb families. The Indian name appeared on the roll of the Cherokee(Lumbee) Indian Normal School catalogue 1936-37. Cited by Jane Blanks Barnhill in SACRED GROUNDS, 2007, a listing of 162 cemeteries in Robeson County. The Lumbee name Spaulding was enrolled at Pembroke State University in 1943.

## Benjamin & Edith Jacobs- Spaulding Family from Bladen and Columbus County, North Carolina

Benjamin Spaulding was born in Duplin County, North Carolina according to the 1860 United States Federal Census of Columbus County, North Carolina. He was 83 year old in 1860 and he died two years later. According to these records Benjamin Spaulding was born in 1777 instead of 1773 as previously stated in other records. Also, these records indicate he was listed as free inhabitants of Columbus County, North Carolina. The 1860 census only had three category for race they were white, black and mulatto. In the 1850 United States Federal Census of Columbus County, North Carolina indicate that Benjamin Spaulding could read and write. The 1860 Census states that Benjamin Spaulding could not read or write . However, this could have been attributed to the aging process. Therefore, this is strong evident that he could read and write before 1850. During 1860 Benjamin Spaulding net worth in real estate was 1500 dollars and 600 dollars in personal wealth. Benjamin Spaulding was discovered in deeds and records as early as 1817. In the Census of 1820, we learn that he is a free man of color. Therefore, we can conclude that he was a free man of color in 1817 and free men of color along with white settlers could own property in state of North Carolina.

Benjamin Spaulding later married Edith Delphi Jacobs a local Native American women living in the Farmer Union Community, which is located in Columbus County, North Carolina. They had ten children between 1810 and 1831, one girl Ann Eliza Spaulding and nine boys, William, Emmanuel, Armstrong, Armstead, John, Iver, Benjamin Jr., David and Henry. (96) The children of Benjamin Spaulding mostly married Native American men and women who most likely were a mix from remnant tribes of Cheraw, Cherokee and Siouan Indians. This is proven thru archeological records which show Native American artifacts in Bladen and Columbus Counties. In the United States Federal Census Report in 1900, in which spouses of the Spaulding Family members are listed in the Indian Census along with Spaulding family members such as Robert O. Spaulding, son of Benjamin Spaulding, Jr., and McIver Spaulding son of Iver Spaulding son of Benjamin and Edith Jacob Spaulding. Also surnames such as Patrick, Moore, Lasewell, Chavis, Sanderson, Locklear, Hunt, Jacobs, Mitchell, Grahams, Blanks can be found in the Indian Census Reports of 1900. This is further evidence that Benjamin and Edith Spaulding descendants continue to married into the Native American Population. After the third generation many of Ben descendants married free African American, whites, and Indians from different tribal regions of North Carolina. Research as shown that we can conclude that the Spaulding Family is a multi-racial family from their origin of ancestry, according to the United States Federal Census and death records.

The Benjamin and Edith Spaulding's descendants have achieved acclaim in all walks of life over the past 200 plus years.. The Spaulding descendants were the driving forces in the founding and success of the North Carolina Mutual Life Insurance Company located in Durham, North Carolina. They have become renowned educators, skilled professionals, acclaimed performers, talented businessmen and women, and successful farmers. Most importantly, the Spaulding descendants have retained their sense of pride and community.(100)

## The State of North Carolina with Native American Ancestry
## (1858 & 1861)
## Willie Jacobs & Delphia Jacobs Descendants

*Lillian Jacobs Moore, Zora Jacobs Mitchell, Lula Jacobs Campbell
Hooper Mitchell, Nashville Moore*

*Lois Webb Jacobs (1891-1988)*

## (1773 – 1862)
### Benjamin & Edith Jacobs Spaulding Descendants

Edith Spaulding Campbell
(1848-1912)

McIver Spaulding
(1857-1937)

Mattie Spaulding Campbell
(1890-1978)

Dr. Major Franklin Spaulding
(1898-1964)

Carrie Spaulding Wilson (1896-1984)

Dow Spaulding (1903-1994)

John & Penelope
Spaulding Descendants

Jonathan Spaulding (1863-1926)
Indian School Teacher in
Pembroke, North Carolina

Fletcher Spaulding
(1898-1994)

Benjamin Robert Spaulding
(1878-1962)

## The Surname Blanks

*A man by the name of John Blanks of mix blood was in Robeson County area by 1774. In the 1775 tax list of Bladen County there was a man by the name of John Blanks, "Free Person of Color." In 1779 he had 100 acres, 3 horses, and 5 cattle. In 1786 he had six blacks and lived next door to Ann Locklear. Another 1789 tax list had him as White. A man named Joseph Blanks was in the Granville County tax list in 1784. Nobody knew what to call the Blanks family. John Blanks, listed as mulatto, was found in the 1830 census of Robeson. John Blanks, age 29 in 1850, said that he was white and born in Robeson County. By contrast, William Blanks, age 48, said he was mulatto and was also originally from Robeson. The name was self-identified as Indian in the 1900 Census of Robeson. Listed in the 1900 Indian Census of Robeson County. The name was found at Lumberton and Rozier in the 1900 Directory of Robeson as "Croatan." Blanks was listed as Indian in the 1930 census of Saddletree Township. Death Records of 1920, 1930, and 1941, show the Indian name of Blanks to have been in Howellsville, Lumberton, Philadelphus and Saddletree townships. A lumbee named Blanks was enrolled at Pembroke State College in 1924.*

## John Blanks Family from Bladen and Columbus Counties, North Carolina

*John Blanks was born around 1750 in Bladen County, North Carolina. North Carolina land deeds first mention John Blanks obtaining a 100-acre land grant on July 22, 1774. This land is next to Abraham Freeman land which is located between the Fork of Fryers Swamp and Slaparse Swamp according to North Carolina land deed dated to Abraham Freeman on October 28$^{th}$ 1765. (101) Later, John Blanks can be found in the 1790 census of the United States of America living in Bladen County, North Carolina, as a free inhabitant with eight other people living in his house. He owned no slaves according to the 1790 census of Bladen County, North Carolina.*

*Milton E. Campbell*

*Elijah Blanks was born in 1808 , and he married Elender Spaulding who was born in 1820. Their children were Samuel Blanks, Abram Blanks, Henry J Blanks, Alfred Blanks, Dennis Blanks, Morganer Blanks, Gustus Blanks, Elijah Blanks, Jr., Joshua Blanks.*
*In the 1850 Census of the United States of America Elijah Blanks appears to be living in Cape Fear South West Side in Bladen County, North Carolina as a free inhabitant. (102) Joshua Blanks was born in 1836 and his brother Samuel Blanks was born in (1839). Samuel Blanks married Emmaline Spaulding in 1865, and Joshua Blanks married a Native American women named Elsey Chavis daughter of Shade Chavis from Robeson County, North Carolina. In the 1860 census Samuel Blanks along with his brother Joshua Blanks were living in Westbrook Township in Bladen County, North Carolina. In 1870 Joshua Blanks had moved to Welches Creek Township in Columbus County, North Carolina. Also in 1870 Samuel Blanks had moved to Carvers Creek Township in Bladen County. According to the 1880 census of the United States of America Samuel Blanks was living in White Creek Township located in Bladen County, North Carolina. Joshua Blanks was still living in Welch Creek Township in Columbus County.*

*John Blanks obtain a land grant from an officer of the King of England in 1774, and that is when we first see the establishment of the settlement of Indian wells which is located on the Cape Fear River just outside of East Arcadia in Bladen County, North Carolina. According to archeologist there has been Indian artifacts and Native American Burial Ground located in this area. Artifacts of the Siouan Indians can be found in the Lake Waccamaw Museum located in LakeWaccamaw, North Carolina. The Blanks family are descendants of the Woocon or Siouan Stock and it is possible that they were mix with Highland Scot as they arrive in Bladen County, North Carolina. According to the United States Federal Census of 1860 Elijah Blanks was born in 1808 and was a free inhabitant of Westbrook township located in Bladen County, North Carolina. He also is listed as a Mulatto a person of mix blood. The 1860 Census didn't include a classification for Native American Indians. The United States Federal Census of Bladen County in 1860 Census classified everyone as*

Black, White, or Mulatto. Native American Indians were often grouped in the Mulatto category since they were not black or white.

Samuel Blanks born in 1839 and his son John Wesley Blanks was born in 1884. John Blanks married Fannie Ester Moore, who was born in 1885, a Native American Women at birth according to United States Federal Census. John Wesley Blank's son John Henry Blanks was born November 19$^{th}$, 1911 and married Jannie Spaulding. John Henry Blanks and Jannie Spaulding created a document in order to preserve their family Native American Heritage. The affiant was made on January 16$^{th}$ 1945 and stated the following.: John Henry Blanks and Jannie Spaulding Blanks are the parents of Fannie Lee Blanks: John Henry Blanks is the son of John W. Blanks and wife, Fannie Ester Moore Blanks; That John W. Blanks the son of Sam Blanks and Emeline Spaulding Blanks; That Fannie Ester Moore Daughter of Johnny Moore and wife Francis Spaulding Moore. That Jannie Spaulding Blanks is the daughter of Ben. R. Spaulding and wife, Christain Sanderson Spaulding; Ben R. Spaulding is the son of Robert Spaulding and Jane Tucker Spaulding, his wife, both deceased at the time of the affiant.. That the parents of Christain Sanderson Spaulding were from Pembroke, Robeson County, North Carolina. ; That the other parties herein mentioned are of Columbus and Bladen Counties, North Carolina; That John Henry Blanks and Jannie Spaulding Blanks live in the Indian Settlement of Hickory Hill: that all of the above names parties are members of the Indian Race. John Henry Blanks and Jannie Spaulding daughter Fannie Lee Blanks and her ancestors are members of the Indian race. Fannie Lee Blanks married Elmore R. Campbell and to the union two children were conceived. Wanda Campbell born January 7$^{th}$, 1959 and Milton Campbell born September 5, 1962. Both are Native American according to birth records located in Columbus and Roberson counties. (103)

John Blanks descendants in the beginning resided predominantly in Bladen and Columbus counties which are two counties located in North Carolina. However, the descendants are located all over the United States. Some of the present day John Blanks descendants are members of the Lake Waccamaw Siouan Tribe with their tribal office located in Bolton,

North Carolina. There are some descendants that are members of the Lumbee Indian tribe with their tribal office located in Pembroke, North Carolina. The descendants of John Blanks understand the importants of keeping the Native American Heritage alive in the 21$^{st}$ century.

## Joshua & Elsie C. Blanks Descendants

Betty Ann Blanks
(1873-1931)

Elsie Blanks Spaulding
(1872-1956)

*Fannie Lee Blanks Campbell*

## The Surname Moore

The Moore surname was self-identified as Indian in the 1900 Census of Robeson. Listed on the 1900 Indian Census Schedule of Robeson County. Moore was listed as Indian in the 1930 census of Pembroke Township. Death records show the Indian name Moore in 1925 in Pembroke and Smiths townships. They were related to the Carters. The Moore name is listed on the roll of Cherokee(Lumbee) Indian Normal School catalogue 1936-37. Cited at Benson's Chapel cemetery by Jane Blanks Barnhill, Sacred Ground, 2007, a listing of 162 Lumbee cemeteries. The name may be white or Lumbee in Robeson County. The surname Moore was the $8^{th}$ most popular in the first federal census of America in 1790.

## The Moore Family from Columbus County, North Carolina

The Moore Family from Columbus County, North Carolina originated from Moore County North Carolina. (104)
The first mention of the Moore Family name in Columbus County was in 1786. This is the year we find that Benjamin Moore, Sr. was born and his wife Martha was born in 1790. They are the parents of John Moore. John Moore married Frances Moore (1839 -1905). Frances Moore was the daughter of Isreal Moore, Sr.(1817-1893) and Ann Eliza Spaulding Moore (1822-1906). Isreal Moore, Sr and Ann Eliza Spaulding Moore had other sibling; Caroline Moore, Lewis Moore, Mary Moore, Calvin Moore, Margaret A. Moore, Daniel James Moore, Israel Moore, Jr., Delphina Moore, Aaron McDuffie Moore, and Annie Eliza Moore. (106) In the United States Federal Census of 1900 in Welches Creek Township of Columbus County, North Carolina there are four names we find in the Indian Census. They are John Moore, Fannie Ester Moore, Lewis Moore and Susanna O. Moore. John Moore who is the son of Benjamin Moore Sr. born in 1786. John Moore later married Francis Moore. Fannie Ester Moore who is the daughter of John Moore and Francis Moore married John Henry Blanks from Columbus County, North Carolina. Lewis Moore married Amanda Spaulding, daughter

*Milton E. Campbell*

*of Emanuel Spaulding. Lewis Moore is the son of Isreal Moore, Sr. born in 1817 and died in 1893. Susanna O. Moore who is the daughter of Lewis Moore and Amanda Spaulding Moore. Susanna Moore married Lewis L. Spaulding from Columbus County, North Carolina. The Moore family are Native American Indians, which originated from the Siouan Indian tribe and the Cherokee Indians of North Carolina according to family historians.*

*Beatrice Blanks, daughter of Fannie Ester Moore and John Wesley Blanks still resides in Welch Creek Township of Columbus County, North Carolina. She is the last living child of Fannie Ester Moore and John Wesley Blanks. Beatrice Blanks-Freeman, a Native American Indian has been instrumental in keeping the Native American history alive by leaving a legacy of Native American history to her children and grandchildren. (105)*

## 1817 & 1822
## Isreal Moore Sr. & Annie Eliza S. Moore Descendants

Dr. Aaron McDuffie Moore  
(1865-1923)

Amanda Moore  
(1849-1914)

*Fannie Ester Moore (1886-1960)*

*Dr. William Luther Moore
(1857-1930)*

# Chapter XIII

## Native American Ancestry

Mattie Spaulding Campbell (1890-1978) born in Columbus County, North Carolina, was the daughter of McIver Spaulding and Elsie Blanks. Mattie spoke often about the Native American Blood in here family. Her Father McIver Spaulding is listed in the 1900 Indian Census as living in Welches Creek Township. His mother was Mary Jacobs a Native American Siouan Indian. Mrs. Mattie Spaulding Campbell mother was Elsie Blanks, whose mother was born in Pembroke, North Carolina. Elsie Blanks parents were Joshua Blanks a Siouan Indian and Elsey Chavis who is associated being a part of the Tuscarora Indian Nation. Mrs. Mattie Spaulding Campbell talked about while being interviewed how the Indian people were discriminated against and called white, black, and Mulatto's in the United State Census Reports. It wasn't until the 1900s that some of these records were changed and other weren't changed due to the social and economical situations of many Native Americans. She said that Native American had to do what every it took to survive against the persecutions and discrimination imposed on them by state laws of North Carolina.

Carolyn Oxendine is a Native American Indian woman who lives in Roberson County, North Carolina. She has been feature as the Indian Story Teller in videos regarding the Lumbee Indians. Carolyn Oxendine was interviewed on August 7, 2010 by Milton Campbell and Wendell Campbell. Mrs. Oxendine is a proud Native American woman who has worked with the Lumbee Tribal Council and with the Tuscarora Indians of North Carolina. She talks about the discrimination and injustice in the Nineteenth Century that the Lumbee Indians faced along with other tribes in the area. Later, she speaks about the discrimination in the Christian Churches against the Lumbee Indians and how they formed their Native American Christian Church after their people weren't allowed to preach in predominant Caucasian churches in the early 1900s.

She spoke about how her ancestors had informed her that the Lumbee Indians were originally called the Hatteras Indians but were incorrectly name the Croatan Indians by the Europeans. This would support the earliest and perhaps most famous theory of the Lumbee tribe's origin is that of the so-called Lost Colony Theory, proposed in 1885 by Robeson County legislator and local historian Hamilton McMillan and later expanded upon by North Carolina historian Stephen B. Weeks. Mrs. Oxendine farther elaborates on Henry Berry Lowry, how he killed the sheriff in Pembroke and was a Native American Hero because he stood up again the white man injustice against the Native American people living in Pembroke,

North Carolina. Lowery disappeared mysteriously in February 1872, and today he remains and important symbol of Lumbee pride and the tribe's authentic Indian identity.

Mrs. Oxendine stated that the Lumbee Tribe consist of more than 50,000 members in 2010 and is the largest of North Carolina's American Indian groups. Also, she informed me that the Lumbee Indians are the ninth largest tribe in the United States. As we proceeded with the interview she further states that today most lumbees live in Robeson County and the adjacent counties of Cumberland, Hoke, and Scotland. According to Mrs. Oxendine, Lumbee Indians that had left the area of Pembroke, North Carolina seems to have made major advancements in eduation, and that most of them became more prosperous than the Lumbees that remained in the Pembroke area .

Mrs. Oxendine speaks of the Descendants of Benjamin and Edith Jacobs Spaulding Descendants and that many of them married lumbee Indians from Roberson County, North Carolina. She discovered in her research that the first Spaulding Descendant that came to Pembroke, North Carolina was George F. Spaulding, who was born in1856 and he is the son of Benjamin Spaulding, Jr, (1824-1864) son of Benjamin and Edith Jacobs Spaulding (1773-1862). While living in Pembroke, North Carolina he married Mary Oxendine. They lived in Burnt Swamp Township of Pembroke, which is located in Robeson County, North Carolina. This information was proven to be true base on the 1880 Census of Robeson County, North Carolina. Their children were Rosa Lee Spaulding, Arthur Spaulding, Tommie Spaulding, Evan Spaulding, William Spaulding, Annie Spaulding, Johnnie Spaulding, and Luther Spaulding. Mrs. Oxendine research shows that the Moore, Spaulding and Oxendine families were three of the first Indian families in the Pembroke Area in which all adults in the household could read and write, according to the 1880 census of Roberson County.

*Milton E. Campbell*

*According to the 1900 United States Federal Census there were 30 members in the household of George and Mary Oxendine- Spaulding. Surnames such as Locklear, Oxendine were found living in the Spaulding dwelling in Burnt Swamp, Robeson County, North Carolina. They all are classified as Native American.*

## The State of North Carolina with Native American Ancestry

Chief Leon Locklear was born on May 10 ,1933, and he stated that he was the Indian Chief of the Tuscarora Nation in Maxton, North Carolina. Chief Locklear and his members originated from the Tuscarora Indians of North Carolina. The Chief's major goals in life his to preserve the rich history of the Tuscarora Indians. The establishment of a Native American Museum and Library upon the Tuscarora Nation has accomplished this goal.

Within the Native American Museum there are many native artifacts that are over 10, 000 years old. The museum also has drums made from cow skin that the chief had made. In additional, there are many maps of Native American land prior to European excursions in what is now called the United States. These maps document the location of native tribes all over the United States.

Chief Locklear was very proud of the Longhouse that he had reconstructed upon the Tuscarora Indian Territory. The Longhouse is a place of worship and to host meeting in order to discuss business. He spoke about the Clan System within the Tuscarora Tribe and that members of the same clan didn't marry each other. Afterward, he spoke of how he enjoyed the Tuscarora Pow Wow where different Native American Tribes came to fellowship.

*Milton E. Campbell*

*Federal Recognition is something that the Tuscarora Indian Chief would love to obtain for his people. This would make the social and economic conditions much better for his tribe. Quoting the chief, he stated " It is a shame that the Tuscarora Indians don't have Federal Recognition and we were one of the first tribes to live in North America". He also stated that the Tuscarora people would not give up the fight for Federal Recognition. In completing the interview Chief Locklear said if he was a billionaire that he would buy has much land as he could for the Tuscarora Nation. Finally, he said that the Tuscarora people always like to give a gift to visiting friends. Therefore, he gave me a small amount of tobacco as a symbol of love, peace , and happiness.*

# Conclusions

*The author hope is that this book will help many Native American families living in eastern and coastal counties in the state of North Carolina begin to understand their Native American Ancestry. It must be state that Native American Indians were the first to arrive to what is called the United States of America, and they survived all acts of extermination and their culture, arts, crafts and traditions can be found over the entire United States.*

*The Native American tribes mention is the document hold yearly Pow Wow's which symbolized unity and preservation of the Native American ancestry. The Pow Wow is a time where different native tribes from all across the United States participate in traditional singing and dancing among their people. They share with old and newcomers alike the spirit that brought them together and the sense of belonging that keeps them together. Basically, this is a celebration of life and thanks to god for his many blessings among his people.*

*This book documents the early formation of the coastal and eastern counties in the state of North Carolina thru the period of ( 1663-1808). The reader is provided with a brief history of the state from the arrival of Native American Indians through the American Civil War and Post-Civil war periods. The author further provides the reader with Native American tribes across the state that are still is in existence in the 21st century. Specifically, concentration is place on the Native American families living in Bladen, Columbus and Robeson counties that have survived despite order of exterminate of all Indian east of the Mississippi by President Andrew Jackson.*

1. ". North Carolina Climate and Geography". *NC Kids Page*. North Carolina Department of the Secretary of State. May 8, 2006. http://www.secretary.state.nc.us/kidspg/geog.htm. Retrieved on 2006-10-07.
2. " The Colony At Roanoke". The National Center for Public Policy Research. http://www.nationalcenter.org/Colonyof_Roanoke.html. Retrieved on 2008-05-23
3. "Annual Estimates of the Resident Population for the United States, Regions, States, and Puerto Rico: April 1, 2000 to July 1, 2008". United States Census Bureau
4. Constance E. Richards, "Contact and Conflict", *American Archaeologist*, Spring 2008, p.14, accessed 26 June 2008
5. David G. Moore, Robin A. Beck, Jr., and Christopher B. Rodning, "Joara and Fort San Juan: culture contact at the edge of the world", *Antiquity*, Vol.78 No. 229, March 2004, accessed 26 July2008
6. Constance E. Richards, "Contact and Conflict". [1], *American Archaeologist*, Spring 2008, accessed 26 July 2008
7. Randinelli, Tracey, *Tanglewood Park* . Orlando Florida: Harcourt. pp.16 ISBN 0-15-333476-2.
8. http://statelibrary.dcr.state.nc.us/NC/HISTORY/HISTORY.HTM North Carolina State Library-North Carolina History
9. Fenn and Wood, *Natives and Newcomers*, pp 24-25
10. Powell, *North Carolina Through Four Centuries*, p. 105
11. Lefler and Newsome, (1973)
12. Paul Heinegg, *Free African Americans in Virginia, North Carolina, South Carolina, Maryland and Delaware, Accessed* 15 February 2008
13. "The Great Seal of North Carolina". NETSTATE. http://www.netstate.com/states/syMbit/seals/nc_seal.htm. Retrieved on 2006-05-12.
14. John Hope Franklin, *Free Negroes of North Carolina, 1789-1860*, Chapel Hill: University of North Carolina Press, 1941, reprint, 1991
15. NC Business History
16. http://civiced.org/index.php?page=timeline_lincoln
17. http://docsouth.unc.edu/highlights/secession.html
18. http://memory.loc.gov/ammem/today/jun08.html
19. http://www.classbrain.com/artstate/publish/NC_civil_war_facts.shtml

20. Fishman, China, Inc.: *How the Rise of the Next Superpower Challenges America and the World*, p. 179
21. Lewis, Rebecca. "The North Carolina Gold Rush". North Carolina Museum of History. http://www.ncmuseumofhisstory.org/collateral/articles/s06.gold.rush.pdf. Retrieved on 2009-04-09
22. http://www.usgennet.org/usa/nc/county/bath/
23. http://www.ussgennet.org/usa/nc/county/bath/slaves.htm
24. "American Fact Finder". United States Census Bureau.http://factfinder.census.gov. Retrieved on 2008-01-15.
25. Find A County (http://www.naco.org/Template.cfm?Section+Find_a_County&Template=/cffiles/counties/usamap.cfm)". National Association of Counties
26. " American Fact Finder (http://factfinder.census.gov/)". United States Census Bureau.
27. http://www.starnewonline.com/article/2008404/News/929624663?Title=Democrats-pick-Huges-to-replace-Wright-in-state-House; " Honoring the Past, Thriving in the Present, and Redefining the Future" Spaulding Family Reunion Book, July 29-August 2, 2010,Page 11.
28. "American Fact Finder (http://factfinder.censkus.gov/)". United States Census Bureau. http://factfinder.census.gov.Retrieved on 2008-02-20.
29. "Parks Canada-L'Anse aux Meadows National Historic Site of Canada (http://.pc.gc.ca/lhn-nhs/nl/meadows/index_e.asp)".Pc.gc.ca.2009-04-24. http://www.pc.gc.ca/lhn-nhs/nl/meadows/index_e.asp. Retrieved on 2009-08-26
30. American Fact Finder (http://factfinder.censkus.gov/)". United States Census Bureau. http://factfinder.census.gov.Retrieved on 2008-02-15.
31. Personal Interview "Fletcher Spaulding", December 1, 1981.
32. United States Census Bureau of Columbus County , North Carolina( 2008).; "Register of Deeds"www.columbusco.org/
33. American Fact Finder (http://factfinder.censkus.gov/)". United States Census Bureau. http://factfinder.census.gov.Retrieved on 2009-02-18; http://www.brunsco.net/
34. Robeson County government official website (http://www.co.robeson.nc.us)
35. American Fact Finder (http://factfinder.censkus.gov/)". United States Census Bureau. http://factfinder.census.gov.Retrieved on 2008-02-18

36. Robeson County government official website (http://www.co.robeson.nc.us) "History of Robeson County"
37. "Robeson Cross Roads Archaeological Survey, Phase I& II Testing in Robeson County," (1993) by Stanley Knick, PhD.
38. "Excavation at the Red Springs Mound, Rb4, Robeson County. Southern Indian Studies XXII: 17-22
39. John R. Swanton, "The Indian Tribes of North America, Smithsonian Institution. Bureau of American Ethnology Bulletin, No. 145. Washington: GPO, 1952
40. Paul heinegg, Free African Americans in Virginia, North Carolina, South Carolina, Maryland and Delaware, 2005(http://www.freeafricanamericans.com).
41. "UNC Pembroke, About UNCP" (http://www.uncp.edu/uncp/about/history.htm). August 22, 2007
42. American Fact Finder (http://factfinder.censkus.gov/)". United States Census Bureau. http://factfinder.census.gov.Retrieved on 2008-01-31.
43. Bishir, Catherine (2005)."North Carolina Architecture (http://books.google.com/books? UNC Press. Pp.38. ISBN 9780807856246.
44. Cowell, Rebekah (2008-10-22). "Carrboro's Founders: People You Should Know ". Carrboro Free Press. pp. 16.
45. Bishir, Catherine (2005)."North Carolina Architecture (http://books.google.com/books? UNC Press. pp.55-56. ISBN 97880807856246. http//books.google.com/books?
46. "Minding the museum" (http://www.chapelhillnews.com/weekend/story/8656.html). Chapel Hill News, July 25, 2007. Retrieved 2007-07-30.
47. McInnis, Stewart (1998-09-24). "Kornegay's research eases livestock impact" (http://scholar.lib.vt.edu/vtpubs/spectrum/sp980924/2b.html). Spectrum (Virginia Tech).
48. Mooney, James(1995){1900}. Myths of the Cherokee. Dover Publications. ISBN 0-486-28907-9.
49. Dr. Robin Beck, et al., Joara and Fort San Juan: Colonialism and Household Practice at the Berry Site, North Carolina, Tulane University, National Science Foundation grant abstract, 7 September 2006.
50. McPherson, O.M. Indians of North of North Carolina: A Report on the Condition and Tribal Rights of the Indians of Robeson and Adjoining Counties of North Carolina, Washington, DC: Government Printing Office, 1915.

51. "Pamphlet". N.C. Commission of Indian Affairs, 1990. Ross, Thomas E." American Indians in North Carolina. See pp. 149-162. Southern Pines, NC: Karo Hollow/Carolinas Press. 1998.
52. " The American Indian and Alaska Native Population: 2000"(PDF), Census 200 Brief. 2002-02-01. (http://www.census.gov/prod/2002pubs/c2kbr01-15.pdf. Retrieved 2007-03-10.
53. Cherokee Indian Tribe. Access Genealogy.(21 Sept 2009)
54. Charles A. Hanna, "The Wilderness Trail" , (New York: 1911).
55. Prentice, Guy, {http://www.nps.gov/history/seac/SoutheastChronicles/NISI/NISI%20Cultural%20Overview.htm"Pushmataha,Choctaw Indian Chief." Southeast Chronicles. 2003 (2008-02-11)
56. Irwin 1992.
57. Mooney, James. "Myths of the Cherokee." Bureau of American Ethnology, Nineteenth Annual Report, 1900, Part I. pp. 1-576. Washington: Smithsonian Institution. (p. 392).
58. Mooney, James(1995){1900}. Myths of the Cherokee. Dover Publications. ISBN 0-486-28907-9.
59. Glottochronology from : Lounsbury, Floyd (1961), and Methuen, Marianne (1981), cited in Nicholas A. Hopkins, The Native Languages of the Southeastern United States.
60. Mooney, p. 32.
61. Drake, Richard B. (2001). "A History of Appalachia". University Press of Kentucky, ISBN 0-8131-2169-8.
62. Gally, Alan (2002). The Indian Slave Trade: The Rise of the English Empire in the American South 1670-1717. Yale University Press. ISBN 0-300-10193-7.
63. Otis, Steven J. A colonial Complex: South Carolina's Frontiers in the Era of the Yamasee War, 1680-1730. Lincoln, University of Nebraska Press, 2004. ISBN 0-8032-3575-5.
64. Brown, John P. "Eastern Cherokee Chiefs." Chronicles of Oklahoma. Vol. 16, No. 1. March 1938.
65. Rozema, pp. 17-23.
66. "Watauga Association". North Carolina History Project.
67. Wishart, David M. "Evidence of Surplus Production in the Cherokee National Prior to Removal." Journal of Economic History. Vol. 55, 1, 1995, p. 120
68. Perdue, Theda. "Clan and Court: Another Look at the Early Cherokee Republic." American Indian Quarterly, Vol. 24, 4, 2000, p. 562
69. Cherokee Constitutional Amendment March 3, 2007

70. 1976 Constitution of the Cherokee Nation of Oklahoma". Cherokee Nation. 1976.
71. United States Census Bureau, Eastern Cherokee Reservation, North Carolina
72. Colonial Records: North Carolina 1890; 768 and North Carolina 1887; 161, respectively
73. Paul Heinegg, "Free African Americans of Virginia, North Carolina, South Carolina, Maryland and Delaware"
74. Blu, Karen I. The Lumbee Problem: The Making of an American Indian People. Lincoln: University of Nebraska Press, 2001. ISBN 978-0-8032-6197-6.
75. Dial, Adolph L. and David K. Elides. The Only Land I know: A History of the Lumbee Indians
76. Hoffman, Margaret M. Colony of North Carolina (1735-1764), Abstracts of Land Patents, Volume I.
77. Thomas, Robert K. " A report on research of Lumbee origins."; Lumbee River Legal Services. The Lumbee Petition. Prepared in cooperation with the Lumbee Tribal Enrollment Office. Julian T. Pierce and Cynthia Hunt-Locklear, authors. Jack Campisi and Wesley White, consultants. Pembroke: Lumbee River Legal Services, 1987.
78. Mitchell, Henry H. (1997), "Rediscovering Pennsylvania's "Missing" Native Americans". The Pittsylvania Packet.
79. Paul Heinegg, "Free African Americans of Virginia, North Carolina, South Carolina, Maryland and Delaware"
80. Forest Hazel. Occaneechi-Saponi Descendants in the North Carolina Piedmont: The Texas Community", Southern Indian Studies, Mathis, Mark A., ed. Vol.40 (October, 1991). The North Carolina archaeological Society, INC., Raleigh, University of North Carolina. The North Carolina Archaeological Society, Inc., Inc., Raleigh, University of North Carolina.
81. Brenda Linton and Leslie S. Stewart, "Economic Development Assessment for the Meherrin Tribe"(http://www.kenan-flagler.unc.edu/assets/documents/ED-Meherrin.pdf.), University of North Carolina, July 2003.
82. F.W. Hodge, "Tuscarora" (http:// www.accessgenealogy.com/native/tribes/tuscarora/tiscarorahist.htm), Handbook of American Indians, and Washington, DC: Smithsonian Institution, 1906, AccessGeneaology, accessed 28 Oct 2009. ; Cusick, History of the Six Nations, 1828.

83. Bruce Trigger, ed., Handbook of American Indians: Volume 15, 1978, pp.287-288.
    Skaroreh Katenuaka Nation (http://www.skarorehkatenuakanation.org/1803affirmancefromUS.html}, North Carolina) Official Website.
84. Niagara Falls History of Power (http://www.iaw.com/~falls/power.html).
85. Sylvia Pate, and Leslie S. Stewart, Economic Development Assessment for the Waccamaw Siouan Tribe(Pembroke, NC: University of North Carolina, 2003), p. 5; and Thomas E. Ross, American Indians in North Carolina: Geographic Interpretations (Southern Pines, N.C.: Karo Hollow Press, 1999), pp.137-140.
86. U.S. Bureau of the Census, 2000 Census of Population, Social and Economic Characteristics: North Carolina(Washington, DC: Government Printing Office, 2003)
87. Pate and Stewart, Economic Development Assessment, p. 9.
88. Martin T. Smith, Archaeology of Aboriginal Culture Change in the Interior Southeast: Depopulation During the Early Historic Period (Gainesville, FLA: University of Florida Press, 1987).
89. For some of the earliest accounts of the Waccamaw, refer to John Lederer, The Discoveries of John Lederer(Ann Arbor, MI: University Microfilms, Inc. 1966) and John Lawson, A New Voyage to Carolina,ed. Hugh Tallmadge Lefler (Chapel Hill: University of North Carolina Press, 1967).
90. For insightful analyses of the Native Southeast's formative post-Contact period, see Alan Gallay, The Indian Slave Trade, The Indians ' New World: Catawbas and Their Neighbors from European Contact through the Era of Re Duke University Press, 1947).
91. Jo E. Aldred, "No More Cigar Store Indians: Ethnographic and Historical Representations By and Of the Waccamaw-Siouan Peoples and their Socioeconomic, Legal, and Political Consequences." M.A. Thesis (Chapel Hill, University of North Carolina 1992).
92. For elucidations of the complexities of race vis-à-vis Native peoples of the Southeast and South, see Peggy Pascoe, "Miscegenation Law, Court Cases, and Ideologies of 'Race in Twentieth-Century America, "Journal of American History 83 (June 1996): 44-69.
93. Ross, American Indians in North Carolina, p. 137.
94. Caldwell, David H., Islay, Jury and Colon say A History Guide, Birlinn Ltd. Edinburgh, 2001.; Colonsay and Oronsay, An Inventory of the Monuments Extracted from Argyll, Vol. 5, Royal Commission on

the Ancient and Historical Monuments of Scotland, 1994.; McNeill, Murdoch, Colon say One of the Hebrides, Reprint, House of Lochar Colon say, Argyll, 2001.
95. United States Federal Census Bladen County, North Carolina 1850; Free Inhabitant in Southwest of Cape Fear River in the county of Bladen, State of North Carolina enumerated on 13th day of September 1850.
96. A Story of the Descendants of Benjamin Spaulding (1773-1862) with Genealogy ; Louis D. Mitchell, PhD and John A. Spaulding ,1989.
97. http://www.theargyllcolonyplus.org/Articles/tabid/161/Default.aspx
98. The Colonial Records of North Carolina.ed. William L. Sanders. 10 vols. Goldsboro, NC, 1886-1890.; State Records of North Carolina. Ed. Walter Clark. XXIV (1918).
99. 1800-1802 William and Sarah Graham Descendants 1999 Family Reunion Booklet; Personal interviews Mrs. Luticia Jacobs, Mrs. Mary Blanks, Mr. Jervey Mitchell, Stedman Graham, Lila Spaulding, Mary Graham, Ruby Campbell, Theresa Blanks, Hattie Spaulding, Geraldine Reid, Meredia Spaulding, Berlene Graham, Hattie Campbell, Josephine Graham.
Spaulding Family Website: www.spauldingfamily.com; Noble Ancestry and Descendants by J,H.Moore (1949).Page: 9-18.
North Carolina, His Excellency Josiah Martin, Esq.: to the Surveyor General order to lay out to John Blanks 150 acres of Land in the County of Bladen on January 19, 1773. Bladen County Deeds Office; File # 2559; Copy of deed was retrieved by Mr. Lamar Iron horse.
100. United States Federal Census Bladen County, North Carolina 1850; Free Inhabitant in Southwest of Cape Fear River in the county of Bladen, State of North Carolina enumerated on 21st day of September 1850.
101. State of North Carolina , Columbus County Register of Deeds: Book RB 966 , Page 67.
102. Noble Ancestry and Descendants by J,H.Moore(1949) Page 8.
103. Personal Interview with Beatrice Blanks-Freeman, Daughter of Fannie Ester Moore Blanks, December 12, 2008.
104. A Story of the Descendants of Benjamin Spaulding (1773-1862) with Genealogy ; Louis D. Mitchell, PhD and John A. Spaulding ,1989. pp.71-76.

Lightning Source UK Ltd.
Milton Keynes UK
UKOW042132191012

**200858UK00001B/37/P**